Mediterranean Cooking

GENERAL EDITOR
CHUCK WILLIAMS

RECIPES
JOYCE GOLDSTEIN

PHOTOGRAPHY
ALLAN ROSENBERG

TIME
LIFE
BOOKS

TIME-LIFE BOOKS
Time-Life Books is a division of Time Life Inc.
Time-Life is a trademark of Time Warner Inc. U.S.A.

Time-Life Custom Publishing
Vice President and Publisher: Terry Newell
Managing Editor: Donia Ann Steele
Director of New Product Development: Quentin McAndrew
Director of Sales: Neil Levin
Director of Financial Operations: J. Brian Birky

WILLIAMS-SONOMA
Founder/Vice-Chairman: Chuck Williams
Book Buyer: Victoria Kalish

WELDON OWEN INC.
President: John Owen
Publisher/Vice President: Wendely Harvey
Chief Financial Officer: Larry Partington
Managing Editor: Lisa Chaney Atwood
Project Coordinator: Judith Dunham
Consulting Editor: Norman Kolpas
Copy Editor: Sharon Silva
Design: John Bull, The Book Design Company
Production Director: Stephanie Sherman
Production Manager: Jen Dalton
Production Editor: Sarah Lemas
Co-Editions Director: Derek Barton
Food Photographer: Allan Rosenberg
Additional Food Photography: Allen V. Lott
Food Stylist: Heidi Gintner
Prop Stylist: Sandra Griswold
Assistant Food Stylist: Kim Konecny
Glossary Illustrations: Alice Harth

The Williams-Sonoma Kitchen Library
conceived and produced by Weldon Owen Inc.
814 Montgomery St., San Francisco, CA 94133

In collaboration with Williams-Sonoma
3250 Van Ness Ave., San Francisco, CA 94109

Production by Mandarin Offset, Hong Kong
Printed in China

A Note on Weights and Measures:
All recipes include customary U.S. and metric measurements. Metric conversions are based on a standard developed for these books and have been rounded off. Actual weights may vary.

A Weldon Owen Production

Copyright © 1997 Weldon Owen Inc.
All rights reserved, including the right of reproduction in whole or in part in any form.

Library of Congress
Cataloging-in-Publication Data:

Goldstein, Joyce Esersky.
   Mediterranean cooking/ general editor, Chuck Williams ;
recipes, Joyce Goldstein ; photography, Allan Rosenberg.
      p.   cm. — (Williams-Sonoma kitchen library)
   Includes index.
   ISBN 0-7835-0323-7
   1. Cookery, Mediterranean.   I. Williams, Chuck.
II. Title.   III. Series.
TX725.M35G65   1997
641.59'1822—dc21   96-29832
                                                   CIP

Contents

STARTERS 15

MEAT, POULTRY & SEAFOOD 41

VEGETABLES, GRAINS & PASTAS 69

DESSERTS 91

INTRODUCTION

It isn't hard to figure out why nearly everyone loves Mediterranean food. Although remarkably diverse, the sunny countries of the Mediterranean share a relaxed approach to living that is reflected in their cuisine, which is uniformly casual and bursting with flavor. Also, with the ever-growing interest in healthy eating, we've discovered that Mediterranean cooking—with its emphasis on fresh produce and complex carbohydrates, and its use of beneficial olive oil—offers us a model worth following in our daily lives.

Most of us had our first experience of such cooking in Italian restaurants. Then, we went on to try the specialties of Spain and Portugal, or Greece and Turkey. Growing bolder, and beginning to recognize the kinship that exists among the region's kitchens, we might have even sampled a taste of the North African table.

In this book, you'll find recipes from all these various cuisines, gathered by outstanding chef and culinary scholar Joyce Goldstein and organized in chapters that will help you plan your own Mediterranean meals course by course. Also featured are step-by-step instructions for basic regional techniques, along with an illustrated glossary of ethnic ingredients.

I have been a great fan of Joyce Goldstein for many years, and can vouch for the fact that she has a true mastery of Mediterranean cooking. She has traveled there extensively and done her research in the kitchens of native cooks. Not surprisingly, then, her recipes authentically capture both the simplicity of the region's methods and the liveliness of its seasonings. Even those dishes that might look a little complicated on the printed page are surprisingly easy to make. I urge you to try them all. You won't be disappointed.

Equipment

General-purpose and specialized kitchen tools for preparing a wide variety of Mediterranean dishes

From measuring cups to mixing bowls, wooden spoons to wire whisks, saucepans to baking dishes, the equipment shown here reflects the techniques and ingredients that contribute to the widespread appeal of Mediterranean specialties. A few items, such as the mortar and pestle and the oil can, convey the unique character of Mediterranean food.

1. Food Mill
Hand-cranked mill purées ingredients by forcing them through a medium or fine disk for coarser or smoother purées.

2. Colander
For straining solids from stock and draining boiled, poached or steamed foods.

3. Paella Pan
Traditional wide, shallow, two-handled pan for cooking the legendary Spanish rice-and-seafood dish.

4. Cheesecloth (Muslin)
Used in double thickness to filter fine particles from stocks and cooking liquids.

5. Sieve
Fine-mesh, sturdy strainer, to be lined with cheesecloth for straining cooking liquid from shellfish.

6. Kitchen Towel
Good-quality cotton towel for general kitchen use.

7. Frying Pan
Heavy stainless steel, aluminum, cast iron or enamel ensures rapid, efficient browning and sautéing.

8. Pot Holder
Heavy cotton provides protection from hot cookware.

9. Saucepans
For simmering stocks and sauces and for cooking small stews and braises.

10. Baking Dishes
Select heavy-duty glazed ceramic or glass for oven-baked recipes.

11. Mortar and Pestle
For crushing garlic or small quantities of other seasonings.

12. Baking Pan
For baking small roasts, vegetables and desserts.

13. Baking Sheets
Resilient sheets of regular or nonstick aluminum, with a rim or without, for toasting bread crumbs and nuts, roasting eggplants, cooking pizzas and general baking.

14. Sauté Pan
For browning or sautéing ingredients, simmering sauces and cooking in shallow liquid,

select a good-quality heavy metal pan. Straight sides about 2½ inches (6 cm) high help contain splattering. A close-fitting lid helps hold in moisture.

15. Ovenproof Pot
Large-capacity enameled metal vessel with a heavy bottom and tight-fitting lid, for use on the stove top or in the oven.

16. Roasting Pan
Heavy, durable metal pan for large roasts and large quantities of ingredients.

17. Sifter
For sifting together dry ingredients in baking and sifting flour before measuring.

18. Assorted Utensils
Crockery jar holds ladle for serving soups; basting brush for brushing filo dough with butter and grilled foods with marinades; rubber spatula for folding; scrubbing brush with stiff bristles for cleaning shellfish; slotted spoon for draining small items from liquids; wooden spoons for stirring; and small and large wire whisks for mixing and beating.

19. Oil Can
Airtight metal can protects olive oil and other oils from exposure to light and air. Long spout is good for drizzling oil.

20. Measuring Cups
For accurate measuring of liquid ingredients, choose a heavy-duty, heat-resistant glass cup. For dry ingredients, select calibrated metal cups in graduated sizes with straight rims that allow for leveling.

21. Pie Plate
For baking whole fruit and other desserts.

22. Condiment Bowls
Small glass or ceramic containers for serving olives, nuts or freshly grated cheese.

23. Kitchen String
For tying stuffed and rolled foods and securing large cuts in compact shapes for even cooking, linen string withstands intense heat.

24. Bamboo Skewers
For holding small pieces of food during broiling or grilling.

25. Measuring Spoons
In graduated sizes, for measuring small quantities of dry or liquid ingredients.

26. Poultry Shears
Sharp, tapered, curved blades easily cut between joints and through bones of poultry.

27. Instant-Read Thermometer
Provides quick, accurate measure of internal temperature when inserted into thickest part of item being cooked.

28. Cutting Board
Choose a good-sized board of hardwood or white acrylic.

29. Peeler
Slotted blade strips away the peels of vegetables and fruits.

30. Corer
Cylindrical blade with serrated edge cuts through fruit to remove core while leaving fruit whole.

31. Spatula
For lifting fish, meat and other foods during cooking.

MEDITERRANEAN BASICS

The step-by-step photographs presented here and on the following pages demonstrate the preparation of fundamental Mediterranean ingredients, along with basic cooking techniques that apply to them. You'll find additional information on ingredients and techniques in the glossary on pages 104–107.

MAKING CLARIFIED BUTTER

1. Melting the butter.
Melt the butter in a small frying pan over low heat. Skim off the froth from the surface and discard.

2. Pouring the butter.
Pour off the clear yellow clarified butter, then discard the milky solids that remain in the pan.

Cheese-Filled Filo Triangles

WORKING WITH FILO DOUGH

Tissue-thin flour-and-water filo forms crisp wrappers for savory or sweet fillings. The techniques described here for layering the dough can also be used for pastries formed with filo sheets and filling layered in a baking pan (see recipe, page 95).

1. Cutting the dough.
If forming filo into triangular pastries such as those on page 15, place the stacked sheets of dough on a work surface. Steadying the dough with one hand, use a sharp knife to cut lengthwise through the dough to form strips 2–2½ inches (5–6 cm) wide.

2. Brushing the dough with clarified butter.
Keep the filo strips covered with plastic wrap to prevent drying. Place 1 strip on the work surface and lightly but evenly brush with clarified butter (see box, left). Stack a second strip on top and brush again with clarified butter.

3. Forming filo triangles.
Place a spoonful of filling near one end of the buttered filo strip. Fold one corner of the end at a diagonal over the filling to enclose the filling and form a triangle. Fold the triangle along the strip until the filling is securely enclosed in the layers of filo.

TRIMMING ARTICHOKES

The large buds of a thistle native to the Mediterranean, artichokes consist of tightly layered prickly leaves concealing tender gray-green hearts and clusters of inedible fibers known as chokes. Before being cooked, artichokes should be trimmed and their chokes removed.

1. Removing the outer leaves.
Keep half a lemon on hand to rub all exposed surfaces as you prepare the artichokes, thus preventing them from discoloring. Trim off the artichoke stem about 1 inch (2.5 cm) from the base. Starting at the base, break off the tough outer leaves, snapping them downward.

2. Trimming the leaves.
When a compact cone of pale inner leaves remains, use a sharp knife to cut off approximately 1 inch (2.5 cm) from the top of the artichoke—or as otherwise directed in a specific recipe.

3. Removing the choke.
Gently pull apart the leaves to reveal the small, prickly inner leaves. Using a melon baller or a sharp-edged spoon, remove the inner leaves until you reach the fibrous choke. Scrape out the choke, taking care not to remove any of the artichoke heart with it.

PREPARING DRIED BEANS

1. Picking over the beans.
First, carefully sort through the beans, removing any impurities such as stones, fibers or discolored or misshapen beans. As you pick over them, place the beans in a colander or strainer. Rinse thoroughly.

2. Soaking the beans.
Place the beans in a saucepan, cover with plenty of cold water and bring to a full boil. Remove from the heat and let stand for 1 hour, then use as directed in individual recipes. The beans will absorb some of the water.

PREPARING SHELLFISH

Debearding mussels.
"Beards," the fibrous threads by which mussels connect to rocks or piers, must be removed before cooking. Firmly grasp the fibrous beard attached to the side of each mussel and pull it off.

Cleaning shellfish.
Discard any shellfish whose shells are broken or do not close tightly to the touch. Rinse thoroughly under cold running water, scrubbing with a firm-bristled brush to remove any stubborn dirt.

STEAMING SHELLFISH

Steaming rates as the simplest, quickest way to cook any shellfish. Using liquids such as wine or stock, along with such aromatic ingredients as garlic, herbs or spices, allows you to add extra flavor to the shellfish as you cook them.

1. Cooking in liquid.
Bring the cooking liquid to a boil in a large saucepan or sauté pan. Reduce the heat to a simmer, add the cleaned shellfish—here, mussels—and cover the pan. Steam until all the shells have opened, indicating that the shellfish are cooked.

2. Removing from the shells.
Using a slotted spoon, transfer the shellfish to a colander set inside a large bowl. When the shellfish are cool enough to handle, pull apart the shells and pull out the cooked flesh, discarding the shells. Remove any remaining beards and discard any shellfish that have not opened during cooking.

3. Straining the liquid.
To use the cooking liquid, which will have picked up flavor from the shellfish, strain it to remove any solids, as well as any grit that was inside the shells. Line a sieve with a double thickness of cheesecloth (muslin), place inside a large bowl and pour the liquid through.

Tomato Soup with Mussels

Preserved Lemons

You must put up these Moroccan salt-cured lemons at least 3 weeks before using them in a recipe, such as braised lamb shanks with preserved lemons and olives (recipe on page 50) or vegetable stew (page 72).

8 lemons (about 2 lb/1kg)
10 tablespoons (5 oz/155 g) coarse salt
fresh lemon juice to cover

Scrub the lemons under running water, then place in a large jar. Add water to cover and let stand for 3 days, changing the water at least once a day or up to 6 times a day. Drain and slice each lemon lengthwise into quarters, leaving it attached at the stem end. Have ready 2 sterilized jars, each large enough to hold 4 lemons. Spoon 1 tablespoon salt into the center of each lemon. Place 1 tablespoon salt in each jar and pack the lemons into the jars. Add lemon juice to cover, then cap tightly. Store in a cool, dry place for 3–4 weeks. Do not worry if a white film forms on the lemons; it will rinse off easily.

To use the lemons, rinse well. Cut each lemon in half, squeeze out and discard the juice, and remove and discard the pulp. Cut the peel as directed in individual recipes. Leftover preserved lemons will keep for up to 6 months stored in the refrigerator.

Makes 8 preserved lemons

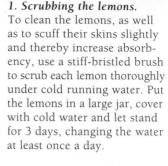

1. Scrubbing the lemons.
To clean the lemons, as well as to scuff their skins slightly and thereby increase absorbency, use a stiff-bristled brush to scrub each lemon thoroughly under cold running water. Put the lemons in a large jar, cover with cold water and let stand for 3 days, changing the water at least once a day.

2. Inserting coarse salt.
After 3 days, drain the lemons. Using a sharp knife, slice each lemon lengthwise into quarters, leaving the quarters attached at the stem end. Gently open the lemon and, using a spoon, insert 1 tablespoon coarse salt into the center.

3. Packing into sterilized jars.
Place 1 tablespoon coarse salt into a sterilized jar large enough to hold 4 lemons tightly. Pack 4 lemons into the jar. Add enough freshly squeezed lemon juice to cover the lemons completely. Cap tightly and store in a cool, dry place for 3–4 weeks.

Tapenade

You can use this Provençal olive purée as a dip for raw vegetables and as a spread on toasted bread. For the true taste of Provence, seek out Niçoise olives, although Kalamata olives can be used in their place and are easier to pit. To pit the olives, hit each one with a meat pounder to loosen the flesh from the pit and then pick the pit out. An olive pitter will not work on Niçoise olives, as they are too small.

1 cup (5 oz/155 g) pitted Niçoise olives
2 tablespoons drained capers, rinsed and chopped
1 tablespoon minced garlic
2 teaspoons drained and chopped anchovy fillet
½ teaspoon freshly ground pepper
4–6 tablespoons (2–3 fl oz/60–90 ml) extra-virgin olive oil
1 tablespoon finely grated lemon zest, optional
2 tablespoons Armagnac or other brandy, optional

*I*n a blender or in a food processor fitted with the metal blade, combine the olives, capers, garlic, anchovy, pepper and 4 tablespoons (2 fl oz/60 ml) of the olive oil and the lemon zest and Armagnac, if using. Process to form a rough purée or paste. Add more oil if the mixture is too thick; it should have a spreadable consistency. Taste and adjust the seasonings, then transfer to a bowl or jar, cover tightly and refrigerate for up to 3 weeks. Bring to room temperature before using.

Makes about 1¼ cups (10 fl oz/310 ml)

Toasted Bread Crumbs

In the Mediterranean, bread is converted into crunchy crumbs that are sprinkled liberally on cooked vegetables, stirred into pasta or used as a topping for gratins.

1 loaf coarse country bread, 1½ lb (750 g), crusts removed
1 teaspoon salt
1 teaspoon freshly ground pepper
½ cup (4 oz/125 g) unsalted butter, melted, or ½ cup (4 fl oz/125 ml) pure olive oil

*P*reheat an oven to 350°F (180°C).

Break up the bread into chunks and place in a food processor fitted with the metal blade. Using on-off pulses, process until the bread is broken up into coarse crumbs. Spread the crumbs onto a baking sheet. In a small bowl, stir the salt and pepper into the butter or oil. Drizzle over the bread.

Bake, stirring occasionally for even browning, until golden, about 20 minutes. Remove from the oven, let cool and transfer to a container with a tight-fitting lid. Store at room temperature for up to 2 days.

Makes 1½ cups (6 oz/185 g)

Tomato Sauce

There is nothing more wonderful than a sauce made with the summertime bounty of ripe, flavorful tomatoes. When good fresh tomatoes are unavailable, substitute about 4 cups (1 ½ lb/750 g) canned plum (Roma) tomatoes.

¼ cup (2 fl oz/60 ml) olive oil
1 large yellow onion, finely chopped
4 cloves garlic, minced
3 lb (1.5 kg) tomatoes, peeled, seeded and chopped
  (*see glossary, page 107*)
salt and freshly ground pepper
pinch of sugar, if needed
2 herbs of choice: 6 tablespoons (½ oz/15 g) chopped
  fresh parsley, ¼ cup (⅓ oz/10 g) chopped fresh basil,
  2 tablespoons chopped fresh oregano or marjoram,
  2 tablespoons chopped fresh thyme

*I*n a saucepan over medium heat, warm the olive oil. Add the onion and sauté, stirring occasionally, until tender, about 10 minutes. Add the garlic and cook for 1–2 minutes to release its fragrance. Stir in the tomatoes, reduce the heat to low and cook, uncovered, until the sauce thickens, 15–20 minutes.

Season to taste with salt and pepper. If the tomatoes are tart, add the sugar. Stir in any 2 of the fresh herbs. Simmer over low heat for 2 minutes to blend the flavors. Use immediately, or let cool, cover and refrigerate for up to 1 week. Reheat over medium-low heat.

Makes 2½–3 cups (20–24 fl oz/625–750 ml)

Pesto

This fragrant green sauce, delicious on pasta, fish or pizza, is the gift of Liguria, Italy, to the food world. If using the pesto as a sauce for fish, omit the Parmesan cheese.

2 cups (2 oz/60 g) firmly packed basil leaves
2 teaspoons finely chopped garlic
2 tablespoons pine nuts or walnuts, toasted (*see glossary, page 106*)
½ teaspoon freshly ground pepper
about 1 cup (8 fl oz/250 ml) pure olive oil, plus extra
  for topping pesto
½ cup (2 oz/60 g) freshly grated Parmesan cheese, optional
about 1 teaspoon salt

*I*n a food processor fitted with the metal blade or in a blender, combine the basil, garlic, nuts, pepper and ½ cup (4 fl oz/ 125 ml) of the olive oil. Pulse or blend briefly to form a coarse paste. With the motor running, gradually add as much of the remaining oil as needed to form a thick purée. Do not overmix; the purée should contain tiny pieces of basil leaf.

Add the Parmesan cheese, if using, and process briefly to mix. Taste and add the salt; you may need less than 1 teaspoon if the cheese is salty. If you are not adding cheese, add 1 teaspoon salt.

Transfer the pesto to a jar and pour a film of olive oil onto the surface, to preserve the bright green color. Cover and refrigerate for up to 1 month.

Makes about 2½ cups (20 fl oz/625 ml)

Cheese-Filled Filo Triangles

1 lb (500 g) feta cheese, crumbled

½ lb (250 g) Monterey Jack cheese, finely shredded

3 eggs, lightly beaten

6 tablespoons (⅓ oz/10 g) minced fresh flat-leaf (Italian) parsley

3 tablespoons chopped fresh dill, optional

½ teaspoon freshly grated nutmeg

¼ teaspoon freshly ground pepper

1 lb (500 g) filo dough, thawed in the refrigerator if frozen

1½ cups (12 oz/375 g) unsalted butter, clarified (*see page 8*) and kept warm

A favorite Greek hors d'oeuvre, these pastries are formed into small triangles, hence their name, tiropetes, *meaning "three-sided pies." Feta cheese can be quite crumbly and salty. The addition of Monterey Jack gives the filling a creamier texture and a milder taste.*

꽃

*I*n a bowl, combine the feta and Jack cheeses, eggs, parsley, dill (if using), nutmeg and pepper. Stir to mix well and set aside.

Place the filo dough sheets flat on a work surface. Cut lengthwise into thirds. The strips should be 2–2½ inches (5–6 cm) wide. Keep the strips covered with plastic wrap to prevent them from drying out.

Preheat an oven to 400°F (200°C). Line the bottom of 2 baking sheets with parchment paper or brush with a little of the warm clarified butter.

Remove 2 strips from the stack of filo sheets, then re-cover the sheets. Brush 1 strip lightly with the clarified butter. Set the other strip directly on top of the first and brush with butter. Place about 1 teaspoon of the cheese mixture on the top strip about 2 inches (5 cm) from one end. Fold the end at an angle over the filling to form a triangle. Continue to fold the dough, preserving the triangle shape, until you have folded the entire strip. Place the triangular pastry on a prepared baking sheet. Repeat until all of the dough strips and filling have been used and both baking sheets are filled. (The pastries can be refrigerated for 1 day; cover loosely with aluminum foil or parchment paper, but do not press down on the pastries or you may tear them.)

Brush the tops with butter. Bake the pastries, one baking sheet at a time, until golden brown, about 10 minutes. Serve hot.

Makes about 48 pastries

Tomato Soup with Mussels

3 tablespoons olive oil

2 large yellow onions, sliced

2 cloves garlic, minced

pinch of cayenne pepper

¼ cup (⅓ oz/10 g) chopped fresh
flat-leaf (Italian) parsley

3 lb (1.5 kg) tomatoes, thickly sliced
or cut into chunks

1 thin orange zest strip, optional

30–36 mussels, debearded and well
scrubbed

1 cup (8 fl oz/250 ml) dry white wine
or water

salt and freshly ground pepper

pinch of sugar, if needed

½ cup (4 fl oz/125 ml) heavy (double)
cream, optional

¼ cup (⅓ oz/10 g) chopped fresh basil
or flat-leaf (Italian) parsley or 6 tablespoons (3 fl oz/90 ml) pesto (recipe on
page 13), optional

*I*n a large, heavy pot over medium heat, warm the olive oil. Add the onions and sauté, stirring occasionally, until tender, 8–10 minutes. Add the garlic, cayenne and parsley and cook for 1–2 minutes to release their flavors. Then add the tomatoes and the orange zest, if using; reduce the heat to low, cover and cook, stirring occasionally to prevent scorching, until the tomatoes have released their juices and are very tender, about 30 minutes.

Meanwhile, place the mussels in a large, wide saucepan, discarding any that do not close tightly when touched. Add the wine or water, cover and place over high heat. Cook, shaking the pan occasionally, until the mussels open, 3–4 minutes. Using a slotted spoon, transfer the mussels to a colander placed over a bowl; discard any mussels that did not open. Reserve the cooking liquid. When cool enough to handle, separate the mussels from their shells, carefully removing any remaining beards. Transfer the mussels to a small bowl and discard the shells. Position a sieve lined with cheesecloth (muslin) over a bowl and pour the reserved liquid through it. Add the liquid to the mussels.

Remove the tomato mixture from the heat and let cool slightly. Working in batches, pass the mixture through a food mill or coarse sieve placed over a saucepan. Season to taste with salt and pepper. If the tomatoes are tart, add the sugar. For a smoother, sweeter soup, stir in the cream.

Place the tomato mixture over medium heat. When hot, add the mussels with their strained liquid, reduce the heat to low and heat through. Season to taste with salt and pepper. Ladle into warmed bowls and garnish each serving with basil or parsley or a dollop of pesto, if desired.

Serves 6

Eggplant and Tomato Salad

3 eggplants (aubergines), about 1 lb (500 g) each

3 tablespoons cumin seeds or 2 table-spoons ground cumin

4 cloves garlic, minced

2–3 tablespoons fresh lemon juice

⅓–½ cup (3–4 fl oz/80–125 ml) pure olive oil

2 teaspoons paprika

¼ teaspoon cayenne pepper

2 tomatoes, peeled, seeded and chopped (*see glossary, page 107*)

3 tablespoons finely chopped fresh cilantro (fresh coriander) or flat-leaf (Italian) parsley

salt and freshly ground pepper

This Moroccan eggplant salad is best made in the summertime, when tomatoes are ripe and flavorful. For a smoky flavor, broil the eggplants. For a milder taste, roast them in the oven.

Preheat a broiler (griller).

Prick each eggplant in a few places with a fork. Place on a baking sheet and slip under the broiler. Broil (grill), turning often, until blistered and charred on all sides and soft throughout, 15–20 minutes. If the eggplants darken too quickly but are not soft, finish cooking them in a 400°F (200°C) oven. (Alternatively, bake the eggplants in a preheated 400°F/200°C oven, turning often, for about 45 minutes.) Remove the eggplants from the broiler or oven. Slit open and scoop the pulp into a colander. Discard the skins and any large seed pockets. Let the pulp stand for about 15 minutes to drain off the bitter juices.

If using cumin seeds, in a small frying pan over low heat, toast the seeds, stirring occasionally, until fragrant, 2–3 minutes. Transfer to a spice grinder and grind to a powder. (Alternatively, transfer to a mortar and grind to a powder with a pestle.) If using ground cumin, in a small frying pan over low heat, warm the cumin, stirring occasionally, until fragrant, 1–2 minutes.

Chop the eggplant pulp coarsely and place in a bowl. Fold in the cumin, garlic, 2 tablespoons of the lemon juice, ⅓ cup (3 fl oz/80 ml) of the olive oil, paprika and cayenne pepper. Then fold in the tomatoes and the cilantro or parsley. Add more olive oil and lemon juice if needed to correct the taste or texture as desired. Season to taste with a generous amount of salt and with pepper. Serve at room temperature.

Serves 6

Dolmas

FOR THE FILLING:

½ cup (3½ oz/105 g) lentils, picked
    over and soaked for 1 hour in water
    to cover
1 cup (7 oz/220 g) long-grain white rice
3 tablespoons olive oil
1 cup (4 oz/125 g) chopped yellow
    onion
½ cup (1½ oz/45 g) chopped green
    (spring) onions
3 cloves garlic, minced
½ teaspoon ground cinnamon, optional
½ teaspoon ground allspice, optional
⅔ cup (4 oz/125 g) peeled, seeded and
    diced tomatoes (see glossary, page 107)
½ cup (2½ oz/75 g) pine nuts
6 tablespoons (½ oz/15 g) chopped
    fresh dill
6 tablespoons (½ oz/15 g) chopped
    fresh mint
¼ cup (⅓ oz/10 g) chopped fresh
    flat-leaf (Italian) parsley
salt and freshly ground pepper

36 grape leaves, preserved in brine
1 cup (8 fl oz/250 ml) olive oil
¼ cup (2 fl oz/60 ml) fresh lemon juice
lemon wedges or plain yogurt

To make the filling, drain the lentils, place in a saucepan and add water to cover by about 1 inch (2.5 cm). Bring to a boil over medium-high heat, reduce the heat to low, cover and simmer until tender but still firm, about 20 minutes. Drain.

Meanwhile, place the rice in a bowl with water to cover and let stand for about 30 minutes. In a sauté pan over medium heat, warm the 3 tablespoons olive oil. Add the yellow and green onions and sauté, stirring occasionally, until tender, about 8 minutes. Add the garlic and the cinnamon and allspice, if using, and sauté for 2 minutes. Transfer to a bowl. Drain the rice and add to the onion mixture along with the drained lentils, tomatoes, pine nuts, dill, mint and parsley. Season with salt and a generous amount of pepper. Mix well.

Briefly rinse the grape leaves, drain well and cut off any tough stems. Place the leaves on a work surface, smooth side down. Place 1 teaspoon or so of filling near the stem end of each leaf. Fold the stem end over the filling, fold the sides over the stem end and then roll the leaf into a cylinder. Do not roll too tightly, as the rice swells during cooking. Place seam side down in a large, wide sauté pan. Repeat with the remaining leaves and filling, preferably placing the dolmas in a single layer.

Pour the 1 cup (8 fl oz/250 ml) olive oil and the lemon juice over the dolmas. Add hot water to cover. Place a heavy plate (or plates) on top of the dolmas to weigh them down. Bring to a simmer over medium heat, cover, reduce the heat to low and cook until the filling is tender, about 45 minutes. Remove from the heat, uncover and remove the plate(s). Transfer the dolmas to platters so they will cool more quickly. Serve at room temperature with lemon wedges or plain yogurt.

Makes 36 dolmas

Lamb and Bean Soup

½ cup (3½ oz/105 g) chick-peas
   (garbanzo beans)
salt
2 tablespoons unsalted butter
1 tablespoon pure olive oil
½ lb (250 g) boneless lamb from leg
   or shoulder, cut into ½-inch (12-mm)
   cubes
2 yellow onions, chopped
2 cloves garlic, minced
½ teaspoon ground ginger
1 teaspoon ground cinnamon
½ teaspoon ground turmeric
6 cups (48 fl oz/1.5 l) water, or as
   needed
⅔ cup (5 oz/155 g) lentils
1½ cups (9 oz/280 g) canned plum
   (Roma) tomato purée or 2 lb (1 kg)
   tomatoes, peeled, seeded and chopped
   (see glossary, page 107)
½ cup (¾ oz/20 g) chopped fresh
   flat-leaf (Italian) parsley
¼ cup (⅓ oz/10 g) chopped fresh
   cilantro (fresh coriander)
1 teaspoon freshly ground pepper,
   or to taste
2–4 tablespoons fresh lemon juice

Lemon is an important last-minute addition, as it lightens the soup and heightens the spices of this Moroccan harira.

❧

Pick over the chick-peas, discarding any misshapen peas or impurities. Rinse well and place in a saucepan with plenty of water to cover. Bring to a boil over high heat, boil for 2 minutes, remove from the heat and let stand for 1 hour.

Drain the chick-peas and transfer to a saucepan. Add water to cover by 2 inches (5 cm) and bring to a boil over medium heat. Reduce the heat to low, cover and simmer until cooked through but not falling apart, about 1 hour. Add salt to taste during the last 15 minutes of cooking. Remove from the heat, drain and set aside. You will have about 1½ cups (10½ oz/330 g).

In a large sauté pan over high heat, melt the butter with the oil. When hot, add the lamb and brown well on all sides, 8–10 minutes. Reduce the heat to medium and add the onions, garlic, ginger, cinnamon and turmeric; cook, stirring, until the onions are soft, about 3 minutes. Add 3 cups (24 fl oz/750 ml) of the water or more as needed to cover the lamb, bring to a boil over medium heat, reduce the heat to low and simmer, uncovered, for 30 minutes.

In a large saucepan over high heat, bring the remaining 3 cups (24 fl oz/750 ml) water to a boil. Add the lentils, reduce the heat to low and simmer, uncovered, for 20 minutes. Add the meat-onion mixture, chick-peas, tomatoes, parsley and cilantro. Continue to simmer for 20 minutes longer. Add salt to taste and the pepper; the soup should be peppery.

Remove from the heat. Stir in 2 tablespoons of the lemon juice. Taste and adjust the seasoning with more lemon juice, if desired. Ladle into warmed bowls to serve.

Serves 6–8

Beet Salad with Feta

4 large or 8 small beets
½ cup (4 fl oz/125 ml) extra-virgin
 olive oil
3 tablespoons red wine vinegar or
 ¼ cup (2 fl oz/ 60 ml) fresh lemon
 juice
1 clove garlic, minced
½ cup (⅔ oz/20 g) chopped fresh mint
½ teaspoon ground allspice
salt and freshly ground pepper
1 red (Spanish) onion, thinly sliced
6–7 cups (6–7 oz/185–220 g) young,
 tender watercress sprigs (about 4
 medium bunches) or baby spinach
 leaves, carefully rinsed (see note)
1 cup (5 oz/155 g) crumbled feta cheese

Popular all over the Mediterranean, salads made with these dense, sweet roots are dressed simply with olive oil and vinegar, tossed in a yogurt-based vinaigrette, mixed with toasted walnuts or, as here, sprinkled with feta cheese. If the beet greens are still attached, they can be cut off and boiled until tender or, if very young, used raw in place of the watercress or spinach.

❧

*I*f the greens are still attached to the beets, cut them off, leaving about 1 inch (2.5 cm) of the stem intact. Scrub the beets well under cold running water but do not break the skin, or the color will bleed as they are boiled. Place in a saucepan with water to cover. Bring to a boil over high heat, cover partially, reduce the heat to low and simmer until tender, 30–40 minutes for large beets or 15–20 minutes for small beets. Drain and add a little cold water to the pot to cool the beets. Peel the beets and slice or quarter, depending on their size. Place in a bowl.

 In a small bowl, whisk together the olive oil, vinegar or lemon juice, garlic, ¼ cup (⅓ oz/10 g) of the mint, allspice, and salt and pepper to taste to form a vinaigrette.

 To soften the bite of the onion slices, place them in a small bowl and dress with a few tablespoons of the vinaigrette; let stand for 15 minutes.

 Add ¼ cup (2 fl oz/60 ml) of the vinaigrette to the beets and toss well. Add the onion and toss to mix. In a separate bowl, toss the watercress or spinach with the remaining vinaigrette and arrange on a platter. Distribute the beets and onion evenly over the greens. Sprinkle with the feta cheese and the remaining ¼ cup (⅓ oz/10 g) mint. Serve at once.

Serves 4

Salt Cod Purée

1½ lb (750 g) boneless salt cod
2 cloves garlic
salt
1½–3 cups (12–24 fl oz/375–750 ml)
   olive oil
1¼ cups (10 fl oz/310 ml) milk
juice of 1 lemon
freshly grated nutmeg
freshly ground pepper
1 loaf coarse country bread, 1½ lb (750 g),
   sliced ⅓ inch (9 mm) thick and
   toasted or grilled

This Provençal dish is called brandade de morue. *The word* brandade *means "something that is stirred." Here a food processor is used to mix the purée, without a sacrifice in taste.*

Place the salt cod in a bowl with water to cover. Refrigerate for 24–48 hours, changing the water at least 4 times. Very thick or very salty pieces of cod will require longer soaking.

Drain the cod and place in a large saucepan. Add water to cover generously, cover and place over low heat. Bring to a simmer very slowly; do not allow to boil or the cod will become tough. Poach gently until the cod is just tender, about 10 minutes. Drain and let cool slightly. Remove all traces of skin and any errant bones. Flake the cod with your fingers or a fork and place in a food processor fitted with the metal blade.

Using the flat side of a chef's knife, crush the garlic. Transfer to a small bowl and use a fork to blend in salt to taste until a fine paste forms. (Alternatively, place the garlic in a mortar and use a pestle to crush the garlic and blend in the salt.) Add to the food processor and pulse once to combine with the cod. In a small saucepan over low heat, warm 1½ cups (12 fl oz/375 ml) of the olive oil. In another saucepan over low heat, warm the milk. With the motor running, add half of the warm oil, a bit at a time, then add half of the warm milk. Continue adding in the warm oil and warm milk alternately. Add as much of the remaining 1½ cups (12 fl oz/375 ml) oil, a little at a time, as needed to achieve a pale, thick, smooth mixture. Add the lemon juice and season to taste with nutmeg and pepper.

Serve the purée at once or transfer to the top pan of a double boiler and keep warm over hot water. Serve with the toasted or grilled bread.

Serves 6–8

Vegetable Soup with Basil and Garlic

½ cup (3½ oz/105 g) dried cannellini
  beans
salt
3 tablespoons pure olive oil
4 yellow onions, diced
6 carrots, peeled and sliced
4 celery stalks, diced
1 lb (500 g) tomatoes, peeled, seeded
  and diced (see glossary, page 107)
8 cups (64 fl oz/2 l) water or chicken
  stock
6 new potatoes, diced
½ lb (250 g) green beans, trimmed and
  cut into 1-inch (2.5-cm) lengths
4 zucchini (courgettes), cut in half
  lengthwise, then sliced crosswise
  ½ inch (12 mm) thick
4 cups (8 oz/250 g) sliced Swiss chard
  (silverbeet), sliced ½ inch (12 mm)
  wide, carefully rinsed
¼ lb (125 g) dried macaroni or small
  pasta shells
freshly ground pepper
1 cup (8 fl oz/250 ml) pesto (recipe on
  page 13)
extra-virgin olive oil, optional
freshly grated Parmesan cheese, optional

Called soupe au pistou, *this is a Provençal mélange of spring vegetables and pasta in a fragrant broth. If the word* pistou *sounds familiar, it is essentially the French version of the Italian pesto.*

Pick over the cannellini beans, discarding any misshapen beans or impurities. Rinse well and place in a saucepan with plenty of water to cover. Bring to a boil over high heat, boil for 2 minutes, remove from the heat and let stand for 1 hour. Drain and return to the saucepan. Add water to cover by 2 inches (5 cm) and bring to a boil over medium-high heat. Reduce the heat to low, cover and simmer until cooked through but not falling apart, about 1 hour. Add salt to taste during the last 15 minutes of cooking. Remove from the heat, drain and set aside.

In a large soup pot over medium heat, warm the pure olive oil. Add the onions and sauté, stirring occasionally, until tender, 8–10 minutes. Add the carrots and celery and cook, stirring, for about 5 minutes longer. Then add the tomatoes and water or stock, reduce the heat to low and simmer for 10 minutes.

Add the potatoes and continue to simmer until the potatoes are tender, about 15 minutes. Add the cooked cannellini beans, green beans, zucchini, chard and pasta during the last 10 minutes of cooking. Season to taste with salt and pepper.

Remove from the heat and stir in the pesto. Immediately ladle into warmed bowls. Drizzle each serving with extra-virgin olive oil and top with a little Parmesan cheese, if desired. Serve at once.

Serves 6–8

Shrimp and Garlic Omelet

¾ lb (375 g) small shrimp (prawns), peeled and deveined (*see glossary, page 107*)

½ lb (250 g) pencil-thin asparagus, tough stem ends removed and cut into 1-inch (2.5-cm) lengths

6 tablespoons (3 fl oz/90 ml) olive oil

1 small yellow onion, finely chopped, or 8 green (spring) onions, including tender green tops, finely chopped

12 garlic chives, chopped

2 cloves garlic, minced

6 extra-large or 7 large eggs

salt and freshly ground pepper

In Spain, this simple omelet, known as tortilla de gambas y ajo, *would be served as part of an assortment of tapas. Garlic chives, flat-bladed chives also called Chinese chives, have a distinctive garlicky taste.*

⁂

*B*ring a saucepan three-fourths full of water to a boil over high heat. Cook the shrimp in the boiling water until they turn pink and begin to curl, about 4 minutes. Drain and set aside to cool.

Refill the saucepan three-fourths full of water, salt it lightly and bring to a boil over high heat. Add the asparagus and cook until tender-crisp, 3–5 minutes. Drain and immerse in cold water to halt the cooking. Drain again.

In a sauté pan over medium heat, warm 3 tablespoons of the olive oil. Add the yellow onion or green onions and sauté, stirring occasionally, until tender, about 8 minutes. Reduce the heat to low and add the chives, garlic, shrimp and asparagus and cook, stirring, for 2 minutes. Remove from the heat.

In a bowl, lightly beat the eggs. Add the shrimp mixture, stir well and season to taste with salt and pepper. In a 10-inch (25-cm) omelet pan or sauté pan over high heat, warm the remaining 3 tablespoons oil. When very hot, pour in the egg mixture and reduce the heat to medium. Cook until the underside of the omelet is golden and the top is slightly set, 5–6 minutes, running a spatula around the edges of the pan a few times during cooking to prevent sticking. Invert a plate over the pan and carefully flip the pan and plate together so the omelet is golden side up. Slide the omelet back into the pan and cook briefly on the second side until pale gold, 2–3 minutes longer. Do not overcook or the omelet will be too dry.

Slide the omelet onto a serving plate, let cool briefly and cut into wedges to serve.

Serves 6

Orange, Fennel and Endive Salad

FOR THE VINAIGRETTE:
5 tablespoons (3 fl oz/80 ml) walnut oil
3 tablespoons pure olive oil
1 tablespoon balsamic vinegar
¼ cup (2 fl oz/60 ml) fresh orange juice
1 tablespoon fresh lemon juice
salt and freshly ground pepper
pinch of sugar, if needed

FOR THE SALAD:
3 large oranges
½ cup (2 oz/60 g) walnuts, toasted
   (see glossary, page 106) and coarsely
   chopped
3 small fennel bulbs
3 heads Belgian endive (chicory/witloof)

Colorful and refreshing, this salad combines tart-sweet oranges, licorice-flavored fennel and slightly bitter endive with a walnut-and-orange vinaigrette.

❧

To make the vinaigrette, in a bowl, whisk together the walnut oil, olive oil, vinegar, orange juice, lemon juice and salt and pepper to taste. Taste and add the sugar if needed to balance the tartness of the citrus juice.

To make the salad, cut a thick slice off the top and bottom of each orange to remove the pith and membrane and reveal the fruit. Working with 1 orange at a time, place upright on a work surface and cut off the peel in thick, wide strips, removing all the white membrane and pith. Cut along both sides of each segment to free it from the membrane, letting the segments drop into a bowl.

In a small bowl, combine the walnuts with a few tablespoons of the vinaigrette and let stand for 10 minutes.

Cut off any stems and feathery tops from each fennel bulb and trim any bruised outer stalks. Cut each bulb in half lengthwise and remove the tough core. Thinly slice each half lengthwise and place in a bowl. Remove the cores from the endives and separate the leaves. Add to the bowl holding the fennel.

Add the remaining vinaigrette to the endive and fennel and toss well. Divide evenly among individual plates and distribute the orange segments on top. Sprinkle with the walnuts and serve.

Serves 6

Tuna and Chicory Salad with Romesco Vinaigrette

½ lb (500 g) tuna fillet, about 1 inch
   (2.5 cm) thick

FOR THE ROMESCO VINAIGRETTE:
1 cup (5½ oz/170 g) blanched almonds,
   toasted *(see glossary, page 106)*
1 tablespoon minced garlic
2 dried red chili peppers, seeded,
   or 2 teaspoons red pepper flakes
1 large red bell pepper (capsicum),
   roasted and peeled *(see glossary,
   page 104)*, then chopped
½ cup (4 fl oz/125 ml) red wine vinegar
¾ cup (6 fl oz/180 ml) olive oil
salt and freshly ground black pepper

3 heads chicory (curly endive)
2 hard-cooked eggs, peeled and quartered
   lengthwise
½ cup (2½ oz/75 g) Moroccan, Gaeta or
   other Mediterranean-style oil-cured
   black olives

Pale-green-and-white chicory is the foundation for this wonderful winter salad, called xato, *a specialty of Barcelona. Salt cod is sometimes used in place of the tuna. The salad is dressed with a piquant almond vinaigrette based on the classic Catalan* romesco *sauce. It also makes a satisfying light main course for three.*

❧

*P*reheat a broiler (griller).

   Place the tuna fillet on a broiler pan and slip under the broiler about 3 inches (7.5 cm) from the heat source. Broil (grill), turning once, until lightly browned on the outside but still pink in the center, 3–5 minutes on each side, or until done to your liking. Remove from the broiler and let cool.

   To make the vinaigrette, in a food processor fitted with the metal blade, combine the almonds, garlic and chilies or red pepper flakes and process until reduced to fine crumbs. Add the bell pepper and pulse to combine. Add the vinegar and purée until smooth. Pour the mixture into a bowl and, using a whisk, gradually beat in the olive oil until the mixture has the consistency of thick cream. Season to taste with salt and black pepper. Set aside.

   Cut out the cores from the heads of chicory and distribute the greens evenly among individual plates. Break up the tuna into bite-sized morsels and scatter over the top. Drizzle the vinaigrette evenly over the salads and garnish with the eggs. Sprinkle the olives on top and serve.

Serves 6

Leek, Celery and Rice Soup with Egg and Lemon

3 lb (1.5 kg) leeks
¼ cup (2 fl oz/60 ml) olive oil
1 head celery including leaves, about
   1½ lb (750 g), trimmed and chopped
8 cups (64 fl oz/2 l) vegetable or
   chicken stock or water
salt and freshly ground black pepper
2–3 cups (10–15 oz/315–470 g) cooked
   long-grain white rice
3 eggs, at room temperature
juice of 2 large lemons
3 tablespoons chopped fresh flat-leaf
   (Italian) parsley or dill, optional

The traditional Greek egg-and-lemon thickener called avgolemono *imparts a tart and rich finish to this delicate vegetable soup.*

Trim off the tough dark green tops of the leeks and the root ends. Cut each leek in half lengthwise and rinse well under cold running water. Chop the leeks.

In a large soup pot over medium heat, warm the olive oil. Add the leeks and celery and sauté, stirring, until very tender, 15–20 minutes. Add the stock or water, reduce the heat to low, cover and simmer until all the vegetables are very soft, 30–45 minutes.

Using a slotted spoon and working in batches, transfer the vegetables to a blender. Purée until smooth, then return to the pot. Stir well and season to taste with salt and pepper. (The soup can be prepared up to this point, cooled, covered and stored in the refrigerator for up to 3 days. Bring to a simmer over medium heat before continuing.)

Add the rice to the soup, cover, bring to a simmer over medium heat and cook for 10 minutes. Meanwhile, in a bowl, using a whisk or an electric mixer set on medium speed, beat the eggs until frothy. Beat in the lemon juice and continue to beat until the mixture is very frothy. Gradually beat in about ½ cup (4 fl oz/ 125 ml) of the hot soup to temper the eggs. Then gradually beat in up to about 3 cups (24 fl oz/750 ml) of the hot soup until the eggs are warm.

Whisk the egg mixture into the rest of the soup; do not allow the soup to boil or the eggs will curdle. Immediately ladle into warmed bowls. Garnish with the parsley or dill, if desired.

Serves 6–8

Pizza Margherita

FOR THE SPONGE:
1 tablespoon active dry yeast
¼ cup (2 fl oz/60 ml) lukewarm water
  (110°F/43°C)
½ cup (2½ oz/75 g) unbleached
  all-purpose (plain) flour

FOR THE DOUGH:
¾ cup (6 fl oz/180 ml) water
3 tablespoons olive oil
⅓ cup (1 oz/30 g) rye flour
3 cups (15 oz/470 g) unbleached
  all-purpose (plain) flour, or as needed
1½ teaspoons salt
cornmeal for baking sheet

FOR THE TOPPING:
2½ lb (1.25 kg) tomatoes, peeled
  (if desired), seeded and coarsely
  chopped *(see glossary, page 107)*, or
  2½ cups drained canned tomatoes,
  seeded and chopped
4 cloves garlic, minced
12–16 fresh basil leaves, cut into thin
  strips
¼ cup (2 fl oz/60 ml) extra-virgin olive oil
salt and freshly ground pepper
½ lb (250 g) mozzarella cheese, thinly
  sliced
¼ cup (1 oz/30 g) freshly grated Parmesan
  cheese

To make the sponge, in a large bowl, dissolve the yeast in the lukewarm water. Add the flour and, using a wooden spoon, stir to combine. Cover with plastic wrap and let stand until small bubbles appear in the sponge, about 30 minutes.

To make the dough, add the water, olive oil, rye and all-purpose flours, and salt to the sponge. Beat with the wooden spoon until the dough pulls away from the sides of the bowl, about 5 minutes. Turn out the dough onto a lightly floured work surface and knead until smooth and elastic, about 10 minutes. (Alternatively, combine the ingredients in a heavy-duty stand mixer and beat with the paddle attachment to combine, then knead with the dough hook.) Shape the dough into a ball, lightly oil a clean bowl, place the dough in the bowl, cover with plastic wrap and let rise until doubled in bulk, about 1 hour.

Punch down the dough and turn out onto a lightly floured work surface. Shape into 2 equal balls and place on a floured baking sheet. Cover with a towel and let rest in the refrigerator for 30 minutes.

Preheat an oven to 500°F (260°C). Generously sprinkle a large baking sheet with cornmeal. On a lightly floured work surface, roll out each ball of dough into a round 9 inches (23 cm) in diameter. Transfer the rounds to the prepared baking sheet.

To assemble the topping, in a bowl, combine the tomatoes, garlic and basil and toss to mix. Spread evenly over the dough rounds. Drizzle with some of the olive oil and season to taste with salt and pepper. Distribute the mozzarella cheese evenly over each round and sprinkle with the Parmesan.

Bake until the crusts are golden, 10–15 minutes. Remove from the oven and brush the edge of each crust with the remaining olive oil. Cut into wedges and serve hot.

Serves 4–6 as an appetizer, or 2 as a main course

Chicken with 40 Cloves of Garlic

4 fresh thyme sprigs

2 bay leaves

4 fresh rosemary sprigs

6 fresh sage leaves

1 chicken, 3–4 lb (1.5–2 kg)

½ lemon

salt and freshly ground pepper

½ cup (4 fl oz/125 ml) olive oil

16–32 cloves garlic, or as much as you
 like, unpeeled

chicken stock, if needed

Don't be alarmed at the amount of garlic in this French recipe. And don't be too literal in interpreting the title. Allow 4–8 cloves per person, and no one will complain. The garlic cooks slowly until it is mild and creamy—perfect to spread on grilled bread. Accompany the chicken with green beans, if desired.

Preheat an oven to 350°F (180°C).

Gather together 2 thyme sprigs, 1 bay leaf, 2 rosemary sprigs and 3 sage leaves and tie securely with kitchen string to form a bouquet. Form a bouquet in the same way with the remaining herbs. Rub the chicken inside and out with the cut side of the lemon half. Sprinkle inside and out with salt and pepper. Place 1 herb bouquet inside the chicken along with the lemon half.

In a heavy ovenproof pot with a tight-fitting lid, warm the olive oil over medium heat. Add the garlic cloves and sauté until they release their fragrance, about 3 minutes. Add the chicken, turn it in the scented oil and position breast side up. Add the second herb bouquet to the pot and cover tightly. Place in the oven and roast until an instant-read thermometer inserted into the thickest part of the thigh away from the bone registers 170°F (77°C), 1¼–1½ hours. (Alternatively, test by piercing a thigh joint with the tip of a knife; the juices should run clear.)

Remove the chicken from the oven and transfer to a cutting board. Using a slotted spoon, transfer the garlic cloves to a small bowl and keep warm. Discard the herb bouquets in the pot and from the chicken cavity. Let the chicken rest for about 5 minutes. Carve into serving pieces and arrange on a warmed platter. Add a little chicken stock to the pan juices if they seem scant, reheat and season to taste with salt and pepper. Drizzle the pan juices over the chicken pieces. Serve the garlic cloves on the side.

Serves 4

Roast Fish with Ratatouille

FOR THE RATATOUILLE:

2 eggplants (aubergines), about ¾–1 lb
   (375–500 g) each, peeled and cut into
   1-inch (2.5-cm) cubes
salt
8 tablespoons (4 fl oz/125 ml) pure
   olive oil
2 yellow onions, chopped
2 cloves garlic, minced
3 red or green bell peppers (capsicums),
   seeded, deribbed and sliced or diced
3 zucchini (courgettes), diced or sliced
   ¼ inch (6 mm) thick
3 or 4 tomatoes, peeled, seeded and diced
   (see glossary, page 107)
freshly ground pepper
¼ cup (⅓ oz/10 g) chopped fresh basil

FOR THE FISH:

3 lb (1.5 kg) fish steaks or fillets such as
   halibut, tuna, sea bass or cod, about
   1 inch (2.5 cm) thick
3 cloves garlic, cut into thin slivers
salt and freshly ground pepper
3 or 4 bay leaves
3 or 4 fresh thyme sprigs
1 cup (8 fl oz/250 ml) dry white wine

2–3 tablespoons chopped fresh basil or
   flat-leaf (Italian) parsley

*T*o make the ratatouille, sprinkle the eggplant cubes with salt and place in a colander. Let stand for 30 minutes. Quickly rinse off the salt and pat dry with paper towels.

In a large nonstick frying pan over medium heat, warm 2 tablespoons of the olive oil. Add half of the eggplant and sauté, turning often, until tender, about 10 minutes. Transfer to a bowl. Repeat with the remaining eggplant and 2 more tablespoons of the oil. Heat 2 tablespoons of the remaining oil in the same pan over medium heat. Add the onions and sauté, stirring occasionally, until soft, 8–10 minutes. Add the garlic and sauté until fragrant, 1–2 minutes. Transfer the onions and garlic to the bowl holding the eggplant.

Add the remaining 2 tablespoons oil to the pan over medium heat. Add the bell peppers and zucchini. Cook, stirring occasionally, until soft, 6–8 minutes. Return the eggplant, onions and garlic to the pan and add the tomatoes. Reduce the heat to low and cook, stirring, until the vegetables are very soft, about 15 minutes. Season to taste with salt and pepper. Stir in the basil.

To prepare the fish, preheat an oven to 400°F (200°C). Lightly oil a baking dish large enough to hold the fish pieces in a single layer with the ratatouille. Make slits ¼ inch (6 mm) deep in the fish and insert the garlic slivers into the slits. Sprinkle with salt and pepper and place in the prepared dish. Tuck the bay leaves and thyme sprigs around the fish and drizzle evenly with the white wine. Bake for 8–10 minutes. Carefully transfer the fish to a platter. Place most of the ratatouille in the dish, set the fish on top and cover with the remaining ratatouille. Bake until the fish is opaque throughout when pierced with a knife at the thickest point, 10–15 minutes longer. Discard the bay leaves and thyme sprigs. Sprinkle with the basil or parsley and serve at once.

Serves 6

Lamb Stew with Eggplant Purée

FOR THE LAMB:

2 tablespoons unsalted butter

1 tablespoon olive oil

3 lb (1.5 kg) boneless lamb shoulder, trimmed of excess fat and cut into 1½-inch (4-cm) cubes

2 yellow onions, chopped

salt and freshly ground pepper

½ teaspoon ground allspice

2 teaspoons chopped fresh thyme

2 teaspoons minced garlic

2 cups (12 oz/375 g) peeled, seeded and chopped tomatoes (*see glossary, page 107*)

1 cup (8 fl oz/250 ml) chicken stock or water, or as needed

FOR THE EGGPLANT PURÉE:

3 eggplants (aubergines), about 1 lb (500 g) each

2 tablespoons unsalted butter

2 tablespoons all-purpose flour

1 cup (8 fl oz/250 ml) heavy (double) cream, warmed

salt and freshly ground pepper

½ teaspoon freshly grated nutmeg

½ cup (2 oz/60 g) freshly grated Parmesan cheese

chopped flat-leaf (Italian) parsley

To prepare the lamb, in a heavy pot with a lid over medium-high heat, melt the butter with the oil. Working in batches if necessary, add the lamb and brown well on all sides, 8–10 minutes. Add the onions and salt and pepper to taste and sauté, stirring, until the onions are soft and pale gold, about 10 minutes. Add the allspice, thyme, garlic and tomatoes and cook for 5 minutes to combine. Add 1 cup (8 fl oz/250 ml) stock or water, reduce the heat to low, cover and simmer until the lamb is tender, 45–60 minutes. Stir from time to time and add more stock or water if needed; when the lamb is done, there should be enough sauce to coat the meat and spill over onto the eggplant. Taste and adjust the seasonings.

Meanwhile, to prepare the eggplant purée, preheat an oven to 450°F (230°C). Prick each eggplant in a few places with a fork. Place in a baking pan and bake the eggplants, turning occasionally so they cook evenly, until very soft, 45–60 minutes. Remove from the oven and, when the eggplants are cool enough to handle, peel them and place the flesh in a colander. Let stand for 15 minutes to drain off the bitter juices. Transfer the flesh to a food processor fitted with the metal blade and process until puréed. Set aside.

In a small saucepan over medium-low heat, melt the butter. Add the flour and cook, stirring constantly, until thickened but not browned, about 5 minutes. Add the warm cream and whisk until thickened, 3–5 minutes. Season the cream sauce to taste with salt and pepper and add the nutmeg. Add the puréed eggplant and Parmesan cheese to the cream sauce, mixing well. Heat through before serving.

To serve, mound the eggplant on a platter or individual plates. Place the lamb stew around the purée. Garnish with parsley and serve.

Serves 4–6

Grilled Shrimp with Charmoula

24–32 large shrimp (prawns)
¼ cup (2 fl oz/60 ml) fresh lemon juice
2 teaspoons paprika
¼ teaspoon cayenne pepper
1 teaspoon ground cumin
3 cloves garlic, minced
¼ cup (⅓ oz/10 g) chopped fresh flat-leaf
  (Italian) parsley
¼ cup (⅓ oz/10 g) chopped fresh cilantro
  (fresh coriander)
½ cup (4 fl oz/125 ml) extra-virgin
  olive oil
salt and freshly ground pepper

FOR THE COUSCOUS:
3 cups (24 fl oz/750 ml) water
¼ cup (2 oz/60 g) unsalted butter
1 teaspoon ground cinnamon
1 teaspoon salt
2 cups (12 oz/375 g) instant couscous

Charmoula is an intensely flavored Moroccan marinade and sauce used on fish and shellfish. Here it flavors shrimp.

Peel and devein the shrimp as directed on page 107, leaving the last shell segment with the tail fin intact. Slip the shrimp onto 8 bamboo or metal skewers: For each serving, hold 2 skewers parallel and thread 6–8 shrimp onto them so that 1 skewer passes through near the tail of each shrimp and the other skewer passes through near the head. Place in a baking pan large enough to hold the skewers flat.

In a bowl, whisk together lightly the lemon juice, paprika, cayenne, cumin, garlic, parsley, cilantro, olive oil and salt and pepper to taste. Pour half of the mixture over the shrimp and turn the skewers to coat evenly. Cover and refrigerate for 2–4 hours. Reserve the remaining marinade to use for a sauce.

Prepare a fire in a charcoal grill or preheat a broiler (griller).

Meanwhile, make the couscous: In a saucepan, combine the water, butter, cinnamon and salt and bring to a boil. Spread the couscous evenly in a shallow, 9-inch (23-cm) square baking pan. Pour the hot water mixture over the couscous. Stir well, then cover and allow the couscous to absorb the liquid, 10–15 minutes.

Remove the skewers from the marinade and discard the marinade. Arrange on the grill rack 4–6 inches (10–15 cm) from the fire, or place on the broiler pan and slip under the broiler about the same distance from the heat source. Grill or broil, turning once, until pink, 3–4 minutes on each side.

Uncover the couscous and fluff with a fork. Spoon onto individual plates. Remove the shrimp from the skewers and arrange on the couscous. Spoon on the reserved sauce and serve.

Serves 4

Bouillabaisse

FOR THE *ROUILLE:*

3 slices coarse country bread, crusts
    removed and bread crumbled
4 cloves garlic, minced
1 teaspoon cayenne pepper
6 tablespoons (3 fl oz/90 ml) olive oil
2 tablespoons tomato paste

2 leeks
¼ cup (2 fl oz/60 ml) olive oil
2 large yellow onions, diced
2 celery stalks, chopped
6 cloves garlic, minced
2 teaspoons fennel seeds, ground in a
    spice grinder or mortar
2 bay leaves
2 fresh thyme sprigs
2 cups (12 oz/375 g) diced plum (Roma)
    tomatoes
2 orange zest strips
½ teaspoon saffron threads, crushed
    and steeped in about ¼ cup (2 fl oz
    60 ml) dry white wine or water
8–10 cups (64–80 fl oz/2–2.5 l) fish
    stock or equal amounts water and dry
    white wine
4 lb (2 kg) assorted white fish such as
    snapper, cod, haddock, bass, halibut
    and/or flounder, cut into thick slices
salt and freshly ground pepper
2 tablespoons Pernod, optional
6–8 slices coarse country bread, toasted

*This is probably the most famous of the Mediterranean fish stews.
It is served with* rouille, *a garlicky sauce flavored with tomato and
cayenne pepper.*

*T*o make the *rouille,* in a blender, combine the bread, garlic,
cayenne, olive oil and tomato paste and process until smooth.
Pour into a serving bowl and set aside to complete later.

To make the stew, trim off the tough dark green tops of the
leeks and the root ends. Cut each leek in half lengthwise and
rinse well under cold running water. Chop the leeks. In a large
soup pot over medium heat, warm the olive oil. Add the onions
and sauté, stirring occasionally, until softened, about 5 minutes.
Add the leeks and celery and sauté, stirring, until softened, about
5 minutes longer. Add the garlic, ground fennel, bay leaves,
thyme sprigs, tomatoes, orange zest and saffron and its soaking
liquid, and cook briskly over medium heat for a few minutes.
Add the fish stock or water and white wine, using only as much
as can be easily accommodated in the pot once the fish is added,
and bring to a boil over medium heat. Reduce the heat to low
and simmer for 15 minutes.

Add the fish, cover and simmer over low heat until opaque
throughout when pierced with a knife, about 15 minutes. Season
to taste with salt and pepper and add the Pernod, if desired.
Remove from the heat. Ladle out about ⅔ cup (5 fl oz/160 ml)
of the liquid from the stew and gradually whisk enough into
the *rouille* mixture to form a spoonable sauce.

To serve, place a bread slice in the bottom of each warmed
soup bowl. Ladle the stew on top, distributing the fish evenly.
Pass the *rouille* at the table.

Serves 6–8

Braised Lamb Shanks with Preserved Lemon and Olives

4 lamb shanks, each about ½ lb (250 g)

salt and freshly ground pepper

3 tablespoons olive oil

2 yellow onions, finely chopped

3 cloves garlic, minced

1½ teaspoons ground ginger

½ teaspoon saffron threads, crushed

1 teaspoon ground cumin

2 teaspoons paprika

1 cup (8 fl oz/250 ml) water or lamb
  stock, or as needed

Peel of 2 preserved lemons, cut into
  thin strips *(recipe on page 11)*

⅔ cup (4 oz/125 g) Mediterranean-style
  black olives such as Kalamata

¼ cup (2 fl oz/60 ml) fresh lemon juice,
  or to taste

¼ cup (⅓ oz/10 g) chopped fresh cilantro
  (fresh coriander)

¼ cup (⅓ oz/10 g) chopped fresh flat-leaf
  (Italian) parsley

This robust Moroccan stew is called a tagine *after the cooking utensil in which it is braised. It is flavored with salt-cured lemons. You can substitute 2 tablespoons grated lemon zest for the preserved peel, although the taste is not the same. Serve the lamb shanks with couscous (recipe on page 47).*

Sprinkle the lamb shanks with salt and pepper to taste. In a large, heavy pot or saucepan over high heat, warm the olive oil. When hot, add the lamb shanks and brown well on all sides, 8–10 minutes. Add the onions, garlic, ginger, saffron, cumin, paprika and 1 cup (8 fl oz/250 ml) water or stock. Reduce the heat to low, cover and simmer until the lamb shanks are tender, about 1½ hours. Check the liquid level periodically and add more water or stock if needed to keep the lamb half-covered at all times.

When the shanks are ready, add the lemon peel strips, olives, lemon juice, cilantro and parsley. Re-cover and simmer for 15 minutes longer.

Transfer the shanks to individual plates and spoon the pan juices, lemon peel strips and olives over the top. Serve at once.

Serves 4

Cornish Game Hens Stuffed with Ricotta Cheese and Pesto

3 cups (1½ lb/750 g) ricotta cheese
   (see note)
½ cup (4 fl oz/125 ml) pesto made with
   cheese and walnuts (recipe on page 13)
2 tablespoons chopped fresh flat-leaf
   (Italian) parsley
salt and freshly ground pepper
6 Cornish game hens, about 1¼ lb
   (625 g) each, or poussins, about 1 lb
   (500 g) each
½ cup (4 oz/125 g) unsalted butter,
   melted, or ½ cup (4 fl oz/125 ml) olive
   oil, or equal amounts butter and olive
   oil, optional
1 tablespoon chopped garlic, optional

For this Italian recipe, use moist, soft "fresh" ricotta. If you can find only dense prepackaged ricotta, pass it through a sieve or whip it with a little milk in a food processor before using. Accompany the hens, if desired, with baked tomatoes with garlic, parsley and bread crumbs (recipe on page 88).

*I*n a bowl, stir together the ricotta cheese, pesto, parsley and salt and pepper to taste, mixing well.

Preheat an oven to 400° F (200°C).

Using your fingers and starting at the cavity opening, loosen the skin from the meat of each bird. Be careful not to puncture the skin. Spoon the ricotta mixture into a pastry bag fitted with the wide tip and pipe the stuffing under the breast skin and the thigh skin. (You can also use a lock-top plastic bag with one of the corners cut away.)

Place the birds breast side up on a rack in a large, shallow baking pan. Sprinkle with salt and pepper. If you wish to baste the birds, stir together the butter and/or olive oil, garlic and salt and pepper to taste in a bowl. Roast, basting every 10 minutes with the butter and/or oil mixture, until an instant-read thermometer inserted into the thickest part of the thigh away from the bone registers 170°F (77°C), 50–60 minutes for the game hens and 45 minutes for the poussins. (Alternatively, test by piercing a thigh joint with the tip of a knife; the juices should run clear.)

Remove from the oven and transfer to a cutting board. Cut each bird in half along the backbone with a sharp knife or poultry shears. Place 2 halves on each individual plate and serve at once.

Serves 6

White Bean Stew with Clams

2¼ cups (1 lb/500 g) dried large white
  beans
2 yellow onions, chopped
4 cloves garlic, crushed
1 bay leaf
2 teaspoons salt, plus salt to taste
juice of 1 lemon
4 medium-sized artichokes, trimmed
  (*see page 9*)
4 tablespoons (2 fl oz/60 ml) olive oil
freshly ground pepper

FOR THE CLAMS:
¼ cup (2 fl oz/60 ml) olive oil
2 yellow onions, chopped
4 cloves garlic, minced
¼ cup (⅓ oz/10 g) chopped fresh flat-leaf
  (Italian) parsley
pinch of saffron threads, crushed
2 teaspoons paprika
1 teaspoon red pepper flakes, optional
⅔ cup (5 fl oz/160 ml) dry white wine
36 small clams, well scrubbed

3 tablespoons coarsely chopped flat-leaf
  (Italian) parsley

Pick over the white beans, discarding any misshapen beans or impurities. Rinse well and place in a saucepan with plenty of water to cover. Bring to a boil over high heat, boil for 2 minutes, remove from the heat and let stand for 1 hour. Drain and return to the saucepan. Add water to cover by 2–3 inches (5–7.5 cm) and the onions, garlic and bay leaf. Bring to a boil over high heat. Reduce the heat to low, add the 2 teaspoons salt, cover and simmer until the beans are tender, about 1 hour. Remove from the heat and discard the bay leaf. Set aside until needed.

Have ready a large bowl three-fourths full of water to which you have added the lemon juice. Cut the artichokes lengthwise into quarters and drop into the lemon water.

In a small sauté pan over medium heat, warm 3 tablespoons of the olive oil. Drain the artichokes, reserving the lemon water, and add them to the pan. Add the lemon water to a depth of 1 inch (2.5 cm), cover and cook, stirring occasionally, until tender, 6–8 minutes. Season to taste with salt and pepper. Remove from the heat and drizzle with the remaining 1 tablespoon oil.

Place the beans over medium heat, add the artichokes and reheat the beans to serving temperature.

Meanwhile, cook the clams: In a wide sauté pan over medium heat, warm the olive oil. Add the onions and sauté, stirring occasionally, until tender, 8–10 minutes. Add the garlic, parsley, saffron and paprika and the red pepper flakes, if using. Cook for 2 minutes. Add the wine and clams, discarding any clams with open or cracked shells. Bring to a boil, cover and cook, shaking the pan occasionally, until the clams open, about 3 minutes.

Spoon the clams and their sauce over the bean stew, discarding any clams that did not open. Heat for 2 minutes; taste and adjust the seasonings. Ladle into warmed bowls, sprinkle with the parsley and serve.

Serves 4

Swordfish with Lemon, Garlic and Olive Oil

⅓ cup (3 fl oz/80 ml) fresh lemon juice
⅔ cup (5 fl oz/160 ml) extra-virgin
  olive oil
2¼ lb (1.1 kg) swordfish fillets, cut into
  1½-inch (4-cm) cubes
salt and freshly ground black pepper
1 tablespoon minced garlic
2 teaspoons dried oregano, optional
1 red (Spanish) onion
18 lemon slices and/or 18 bay leaves,
  plus lemon slices for garnish

In Greece, Turkey and Sicily, swordfish is greatly prized. While it is prepared in innumerable ways, grilling it on skewers is among the most popular. This recipe, which is enjoyed with variations in all of those locales, seasons the fish with lemon and garlic. Serve with rice pilaf or roast potatoes, and broccoli, cauliflower, zucchini or eggplant.

*I*n a bowl, combine the lemon juice and olive oil. Place the fish cubes in a shallow dish and sprinkle with salt and pepper to taste. Pour about ⅓ cup (3 fl oz/80 ml) of the lemon juice mixture over the fish and toss to coat evenly; cover and refrigerate for 2–4 hours. To the remaining olive oil and lemon mixture add the garlic and the oregano, if using. Set aside to use as a sauce.

Preheat a broiler (griller) or prepare a fire in a charcoal grill. Metal or bamboo skewers can be used; if using bamboo, soak in water to cover for 20–30 minutes and drain.

Cut the onion through the stem end into quarters and separate each quarter into individual "leaves" or thin pieces. Alternate the swordfish cubes with the onion pieces and 18 lemon slices and/or bay leaves on 6 skewers. Arrange the skewers on a broiler pan and slip under the broiler 4–6 inches (10–15 cm) from the heat source, or place on the grill rack. Broil or grill, turning once, until the fish is opaque throughout when pierced with the tip of a knife, about 3 minutes on each side. Serve hot, garnished with lemon slices and accompanied by the reserved sauce.

Serves 6

Leg of Lamb with Yogurt Sauce

1 leg of lamb, 5–6 lbs (2.5–3 kg),
   trimmed of excess fat
4 cloves garlic, cut into slivers

FOR THE MARINADE:
1 tablespoon minced garlic
3 tablespoons dried oregano
juice of 2 lemons (about ½ cup/4 fl oz/
   125 ml)
½ cup (4 fl oz/125 ml) extra-virgin
   olive oil
1 cup (8 fl oz/250 ml) dry red wine
salt and freshly ground pepper

FOR THE YOGURT SAUCE:
2 cups (1 lb/500 g) plain yogurt
1 small cucumber, peeled, halved
   lengthwise, seeded and coarsely grated
salt
2 large cloves garlic, minced
2 tablespoons pure olive oil
2 tablespoons fresh lemon juice
3 tablespoons chopped fresh mint
freshly ground pepper

fresh mint sprigs, optional

Using a sharp knife, make incisions ½ inch (12 mm) deep all over the surface of the leg of lamb. Insert the garlic slivers into the slits.

To make the marinade, in a bowl, whisk together the minced garlic, oregano, lemon juice, olive oil, wine and salt and plenty of pepper to taste. Place the lamb in a nonaluminum container and pour the marinade over it. Turn the lamb in the marinade to coat evenly. Cover and refrigerate overnight.

To make the yogurt sauce, line a sieve with cheesecloth (muslin) and place over a bowl. Spoon the yogurt into the sieve, cover and refrigerate for at least 4–6 hours or as long as overnight.

Preheat an oven to 375°F (190°C).

Remove the meat from the marinade, reserving the marinade. Sprinkle the lamb with salt and pepper and place in a roasting pan. Roast, basting occasionally with the reserved marinade, until an instant-read thermometer inserted into the thickest portion away from the bone registers 120°–125°F (49°–51°C) for rare or 130°–135°F (54°–57°C) for medium-rare, 1–1¼ hours. (Alternatively, cut into the meat with a sharp knife; it should be red or pink, or done to your liking.)

Meanwhile, finish making the sauce: Place the grated cucumber in a sieve set over a bowl, sprinkle with salt and let drain for 30 minutes. Rinse off the salt and squeeze the cucumber dry. In a bowl, combine the drained yogurt, garlic and olive oil. Fold in the cucumber. Stir in the lemon juice and chopped mint and season to taste with salt and pepper. Cover and refrigerate until serving.

When the lamb is done, transfer it to a cutting board, cover loosely with aluminum foil and let rest for 5–10 minutes before carving. Slice, arrange on a warmed platter and garnish with mint sprigs, if desired. Serve at once with the sauce.

Serves 6

Beef with Tomatoes and Oregano

1½ lb (750 g) rib-eye steak or other
   tender cut, sliced ⅓ inch (9 mm)
   thick
salt and freshly ground pepper
2 tablespoons olive oil
1½ lb (750 g) fresh tomatoes, peeled,
   seeded and diced (see glossary,
   page 107), or 2 cups (12 oz/375 g)
   canned plum (Roma) tomatoes,
   preferably in purée, diced
4 cloves garlic, minced
1 tablespoon dried oregano
¼ teaspoon minced anchovy fillet,
   optional
½ cup (4 fl oz/125 ml) dry white wine,
   optional

The name of this Neapolitan specialty, bistecca alla pizzaiola, refers to cooking slices of beef with a classic pizza-style sauce. The sauce is equally delicious with veal or pounded chicken or turkey breasts. Serve with mashed potatoes.

❋

*P*lace the beef slices between 2 sheets of plastic wrap. Using a meat pounder, pound the meat to an even ¼ inch (6 mm) thickness. Using a sharp knife, cut away any sinews. Lay each slice flat and make small cuts around the edge, spaced about 1 inch (2.5 cm) apart, to prevent the slices from curling in the pan. Sprinkle the beef slices with salt and pepper to taste.

In a large frying pan over high heat, warm the olive oil. When hot, working in batches if necessary, add the slices and quickly sear on both sides, turning once, about 3 minutes on each side. Transfer the beef to a platter and set aside.

To the oil remaining in the pan, add the tomatoes, garlic and oregano and the anchovy and wine, if using. Bring to a boil over high heat. Reduce the heat to low and simmer, uncovered, until the tomatoes are reduced to a chunky purée, 8–10 minutes.

Return the beef to the pan and simmer briefly in the sauce to heat through. Serve immediately.

Serves 4

Shellfish with Romesco Sauce

FOR THE *ROMESCO* SAUCE:

¾ cup (6 fl oz/180 ml) olive oil

1 large slice coarse country bread,
  about 1 oz (30 g)

¾ cup (4 oz/125 g) blanched almonds,
  toasted (*see glossary, page 106*)

½–1 teaspoon cayenne pepper

2–3 teaspoons minced garlic

1 large red bell pepper (capsicum),
  roasted and peeled (*see glossary,
  page 104*)

1 large tomato, peeled, seeded and
  diced (*see glossary, page 107*)

1 teaspoon paprika

salt and freshly ground pepper

¼ cup (2 fl oz/60 ml) red wine vinegar,
  or as needed

2 live lobsters and 16 large shrimp
  (prawns) or scallops

olive oil

lemon wedges

To make the *romesco* sauce, in a sauté pan over medium heat, warm 3 tablespoons of the olive oil. Add the bread and fry on both sides until golden, about 4 minutes. Roughly break up and place in a blender. Add the almonds, ½ teaspoon cayenne and 2 teaspoons garlic. Pulse briefly to combine. Add the roasted pepper, tomato, paprika and salt and pepper to taste. Process to form a chunky paste. Add the ¼ cup (2 fl oz/60 ml) vinegar and pulse once. With the motor running, slowly add the remaining oil in a thin, steady stream, processing until the mixture emulsifies. Taste and adjust the seasonings. Transfer to a bowl.

Prepare a fire in a charcoal grill. Use 8 bamboo or metal skewers; if using bamboo, soak in water to cover for 20–30 minutes, then drain.

Fill a large pot three-fourths full with water, salt it well and bring to a boil. Drop in the lobsters, immersing completely, and cook for 6 minutes. Set aside to cool. Lay each lobster, underside down, on a cutting board. Insert a knife where the body meets the tail and cut the tail in half lengthwise. Turn the lobster and cut toward the head, cutting the lobster into 2 pieces. Remove the dark intestinal vein, the gravelly sac at the head and any other organs and discard. Using a mallet, crack the claws and knuckles. If using shrimp, peel and devein as directed on page 107, leaving the last shell segment with the tail fin intact. Thread the shrimp or scallops onto the skewers.

Brush all the shellfish with olive oil. Arrange on the grill rack, with the lobster halves cut side down, 4–6 inches (10–15 cm) from the fire. Grill, turning once. The lobster meat should be firm to the touch within 6–8 minutes total. The shrimp should be pink within 3–4 minutes; the scallops should be opaque throughout and firm to the touch within about 6 minutes. Transfer to a platter. Serve with the lemon wedges and sauce on the side.

Serves 4

Mussel and Potato Gratin

8–12 small red potatoes, 1–1¼ lb
  (500–625 g)

½ cup (4 fl oz/125 ml) olive oil

salt and freshly ground pepper

2 cups (8 oz/250 g) diced yellow onion

5–6 lb (2.5–3 kg) mussels, debearded
  and well scrubbed

1⅓ cups (11 fl oz/345 ml) dry white wine

2 tablespoons minced garlic

½ cup (¾ oz/20 g) chopped flat-leaf
  (Italian) parsley

1 cup (4 oz/125 g) toasted bread crumbs
  (*recipe on page 12*)

½ cup (2 oz/60 g) freshly grated pecorino
  or Parmesan cheese

Preheat an oven to 375°F (190°C).

Place the potatoes in a roasting pan and rub with a little of the olive oil. Sprinkle to taste with salt and pepper. Roast until the potatoes are tender but firm when pierced with a skewer, 45–50 minutes. Do not to allow them to become too soft; they must be firm enough to slice and still keep their shape. Remove from the oven. Reduce the oven temperature to 350°F (180°C). Oil four individual baking dishes.

In a sauté pan over medium heat, warm ¼ cup (2 fl oz/ 60 ml) of the olive oil. Add the onion and sauté, stirring occasionally, until tender, 8–10 minutes. Remove from the heat.

Place the mussels in a large, wide saucepan, discarding any that do not close tightly when touched. Add the wine, cover and place over high heat. Cook, shaking the pan occasionally, until the mussels open, 3–4 minutes. Using a slotted spoon, transfer the mussels to a colander; discard any that did not open and reserve the cooking liquid. When cool enough to handle, separate the mussels from their shells, carefully removing any remaining beards. Transfer the mussels to a small bowl and discard the shells. Position a sieve lined with cheesecloth (muslin) over a bowl and pour the reserved liquid through it. Add the liquid to the mussels. Refrigerate until serving time.

Slice the potatoes about ⅓ inch (9 mm) thick. Place in a bowl and toss with the remaining olive oil; sprinkle lightly with salt and pepper. Layer one-fourth of the potatoes in each prepared dish. Top with the onions. Using a slotted spoon, transfer the mussels to the dishes, dividing evenly. Drizzle ⅓ cup (3 fl oz/ 80 ml) of the mussel liquid over each dish. In a small bowl, stir together the garlic, parsley, bread crumbs and cheese. Sprinkle evenly over the tops of the dishes. Bake until browned and bubbly on top, 10–15 minutes. Serve at once.

Serves 4

Roast Pork with Figs

FOR THE FIGS:

1 lb (500 g) dried black Mission figs
1 cup (8 fl oz/250 ml) dry sherry
2 lemon slices
1 cinnamon stick, about 2 inches (5 cm)
   long
2 whole cloves

1 center-cut boneless pork loin, 3 lb
   (1.5 kg), trimmed of excess fat
salt and freshly ground pepper
1 teaspoon ground cinnamon

FOR THE BASTING MIXTURE:

½ cup (4 fl oz/125 ml) fresh orange juice
¼ cup (3 oz/90 g) honey
½ cup (4 fl oz/125 ml) dry sherry

FOR THE SAUCE:

3 tablespoons unsalted butter
1 large yellow onion, chopped
3 cloves garlic, minced
1 cup (8 fl oz/250 ml) dry sherry
1 cup (8 fl oz/250 ml) chicken stock
½ cup (2 oz/60 g) ground toasted almonds
   (*see glossary, page 106*)
1 tablespoon grated orange zest
½ teaspoon ground cinnamon, or to taste
salt and freshly ground pepper

6–8 orange slices, optional

*T*o prepare the figs, in a saucepan, combine the figs, sherry, lemon slices, cinnamon stick, cloves and enough hot water to cover the figs. Place over medium heat and bring to a simmer. Cook until the figs are tender, 10–15 minutes. Remove from the heat and set aside for 1–2 hours. Drain the figs, reserving the cooking liquid; discard the lemon slices, cinnamon stick and cloves. Cut the figs in half and set aside.

Preheat an oven to 400°F (200°C).

Rub the pork loin all over with salt and pepper to taste and the ground cinnamon. Place on a rack in a roasting pan.

To make the basting mixture, in a small bowl, stir together the orange juice, honey and sherry.

Roast the pork, basting every 10 minutes with the orange juice mixture, until an instant-read thermometer inserted into the center of the loin registers 147°F (64°C), or the meat is pale pink when cut into at the thickest portion, about 1 hour.

Meanwhile, make the sauce: In a sauté pan over medium heat, melt the butter. Add the onion and sauté, stirring occasionally, until softened, 8–10 minutes. Add the garlic and cook for 3 minutes to release its flavor. Add the sherry, stock, almonds, orange zest, ½ teaspoon cinnamon and reserved fig juices, raise the heat to high and cook until thickened, 8–10 minutes. Taste and add more cinnamon if desired. Add the figs and heat through. Season to taste with salt and pepper.

Remove the pork from the oven and transfer to a cutting board. Cover loosely with aluminum foil and let rest for 5–10 minutes. Slice the pork and arrange on a warmed platter. Spoon the sauce over the pork, surround with figs and garnish with orange slices, if desired. Serve at once.

Serves 4

Artichokes with Mint and Garlic

4 medium-sized artichokes
3 cloves garlic, minced
¼ cup (⅓ oz/10 g) chopped fresh flat-leaf (Italian) parsley
⅓ cup (½ oz/15 g) chopped fresh mint, plus 2 fresh mint sprigs for garnish
1 cup (4 oz/125 g) toasted bread crumbs (*recipe on page 12*)
salt and freshly ground pepper
¼ cup (2 fl oz/60 ml) extra-virgin olive oil
pure olive oil for cooking

In this classic Roman dish, artichokes are stuffed with a savory mixture of garlic, parsley, mint and bread crumbs, and then are cooked in olive oil. If you like, add a few teaspoons minced anchovy fillet to the stuffing mixture.

Working with 1 artichoke at a time, cut off the stem even with the base. Break off all the tough outer leaves. Pull the leaves apart to expose the center and, using a melon baller or a sharp spoon, scoop out the prickly choke.

Preheat an oven to 325°F (165°C).

In a small bowl, stir together the garlic, parsley, chopped mint and bread crumbs. Season to taste with salt and pepper. Add a little of the extra-virgin olive oil and mix well to combine; the stuffing should be crumbly but moist. Tuck the stuffing into the center of the artichokes, dividing it evenly. Tightly close the leaves over the filling. Place stem end down in a baking dish with a lid. Sprinkle with salt and add a mixture of 1 part water and 2 parts pure olive oil to reach two-thirds of the way up the sides of the artichokes. Cover, place in the oven and cook until the artichokes are tender when pierced with a knife, 45–60 minutes.

Transfer to a serving platter or individual plates, drizzle with the remaining extra-virgin olive oil and garnish with mint sprigs. Serve warm or at room temperature.

Serves 4

Pasta with Cauliflower, Pine Nuts and Raisins

1 lb (500 g) cauliflower

¼ cup (2 fl oz/60 ml) olive oil

1 yellow onion, chopped

2 cloves garlic, finely minced (optional)

½ teaspoon saffron threads, crushed
   and steeped in ½ cup (4 fl oz/125 ml)
   dry white wine

6 anchovy fillets, finely chopped

1 lb (500 g) dried penne or rigatoni

⅓ cup (2 oz/60 g) raisins, soaked in hot
   water to cover for 10 minutes and
   drained

⅓ cup (2 oz/60 g) pine nuts, toasted
   (see glossary, page 106)

freshly grated pecorino cheese, optional

The Arabic influence on this Italian pasta is evident in the use of raisins, pine nuts and saffron. Toasted bread crumbs (recipe on page 12) can be used in place of the pecorino cheese.

❧

*F*ill a large pot three-fourths full with water, salt it lightly and bring to a boil over high heat.

Break the florets off the cauliflower stalks. Cut any large florets in half; the florets should all be of uniform size. Discard the stalks or reserve for another use. Add the cauliflower to the boiling water and cook until tender but not falling apart, 5–7 minutes. Using a slotted spoon, transfer to a bowl and set aside. Save the cooking water for cooking the pasta.

In a large sauté pan over medium heat, warm the olive oil. Add the onion and the garlic, if using, and sauté, stirring occasionally, until pale gold, about 10 minutes. Add the saffron and its soaking liquid and the anchovies and cook for 3 minutes to blend the flavors.

While the sauce is cooking, return the water to a boil, add the pasta, stir well and cook until *al dente* (tender but firm to the bite), about 10 minutes or according to package directions.

Add the cauliflower, raisins and pine nuts to the onions along with a ladleful of the pasta water. Simmer over low heat until the florets are very soft, 3–4 minutes.

Scoop out a little more pasta water and set aside. Drain the pasta and place in a large warmed bowl. Add the sauce and toss well. If the mixture seems a little dry, add some of the reserved pasta water and toss again. Serve at once with the pecorino cheese, if desired.

Serves 4–6

Vegetable Stew

This tasty North African vegetable stew served over couscous (recipe on page 47) is a meal in itself.

juice of 1 large lemon

6 medium-sized artichokes

5 tablespoons (3 fl oz/80 ml) olive oil

salt and freshly ground black pepper

1½ cups (6 oz/185 g) cut-up green
  beans (1½-inch/4-cm lengths)

2 cups (10 oz/315 g) peeled and cut-up
  carrots (1-inch/2.5-cm chunks)

2 cups (10 oz/315 g) cut-up zucchini
  (courgettes) (1-inch/2.5-cm chunks)

1 large yellow onion, chopped

3 cloves garlic, minced

1 tablespoon ground coriander

2 teaspoons freshly ground black pepper

2 teaspoons paprika

2 teaspoons ground cumin

1 teaspoon ground ginger

½ teaspoon cayenne pepper

2 cups (12 oz/375 g) peeled, seeded and
  diced tomatoes (*see glossary, page 107*)

4 tablespoons (⅓ oz/10 g) each chopped
  fresh cilantro (fresh coriander) and
  chopped fresh flat-leaf (Italian) parsley

2 tablespoons chopped preserved lemon
  peel (*recipe on page 11*) or finely grated
  zest of 2 lemons

1 cup (8 fl oz/250 ml) vegetable stock
  or water, or as needed

1½ cups (10½ oz/330 g) drained canned
  chick-peas (garbanzo beans)

⅔ cup (4 oz/125 g) raisins, soaked in
  hot water for 10 minutes and drained

*F*ill a large bowl three-fourths full of water and add half of the lemon juice. Trim the artichokes as directed on page 9. Cut each artichoke lengthwise into sixths and drop into the lemon water. In a sauté pan over medium heat, warm 2 tablespoons of the olive oil. Drain the artichokes and add to the pan along with 1 cup (8 fl oz/250 ml) water and the remaining lemon juice. Cook, stirring, until tender and the liquid has been absorbed, 6–8 minutes. Season to taste with salt and pepper.

Fill a large saucepan three-fourths full with water, salt it lightly and bring to a boil. Add the green beans and cook until tender-crisp, about 5 minutes. Transfer to a bowl of cold water to halt the cooking. Drain. Repeat with the carrots and zucchini. The carrots should cook in 8–10 minutes, the zucchini in 3–5 minutes.

In a large sauté pan over medium heat, warm the remaining 3 tablespoons olive oil. Add the onion and sauté, stirring occasionally, until tender, 8–10 minutes. Add the garlic, coriander, 2 teaspoons black pepper, paprika, cumin, ginger and cayenne and cook for 2 minutes. Add the tomatoes, 2 tablespoons each of the cilantro and parsley, the lemon peel or zest, and the 1 cup (8 fl oz/250 ml) stock or water. Simmer until the flavors are blended, about 5 minutes. Add the chick-peas, artichokes, green beans, carrots, zucchini and raisins. Simmer until heated through, adding more stock or water if the mixture is too dry. Season to taste with salt and pepper. Transfer to a serving dish and garnish with the remaining cilantro and parsley.

Serves 6

Eggplant Parmigiana

3 eggplants (aubergines), about 1 lb (500 g) each

salt

olive oil for sautéing

1 yellow onion, thinly sliced

2 cups (12 oz/375 g) peeled, seeded and diced tomatoes (*see glossary, page 107*)

2 cloves garlic, minced (optional)

salt and freshly ground pepper

2 or 3 hard-cooked eggs, peeled and sliced

½ cup (2 oz/60 g) freshly grated pecorino cheese

½ cup (2 oz/60 g) fine dried bread crumbs

This version of eggplant parmigiana from Calabria includes hard-cooked eggs. It is ideal for entertaining, as it can be assembled in advance and slipped into the oven just before serving. It reheats well, too.

✦

Peel the eggplants and cut crosswise into slices about ½ inch (12 mm) thick. Sprinkle the slices with salt and place in a colander. Let stand for 30 minutes to drain off the bitter juices. Rinse and pat dry with paper towels.

Preheat an oven to 400°F (200°C).

In a large sauté pan, preferably nonstick, pour in olive oil to a depth of ¼ inch (6 mm). Place over medium-high heat. Working in batches, add the eggplant slices and sauté, turning once, until very lightly browned and translucent, about 4 minutes on each side. Transfer to paper towels to drain. Add more oil to the pan only as needed to prevent sticking; the eggplant will "drink" more than it needs. Add the onion to the oil remaining in the pan and cook over medium heat, stirring, until softened, about 5 minutes. Add the tomatoes and the garlic, if using, and cook, stirring occasionally, until the tomatoes achieve a saucelike consistency, about 10 minutes. Season to taste with salt and pepper.

Spread one-third of the tomato sauce on the bottom of an 8½-by-12-inch (21.5-by-30-cm) baking dish with 2-inch (5-cm) sides. Top with half of the eggplant slices. Spread half of the remaining sauce over the eggplant; layer on half of the eggs and then the remaining eggplant. Top with the remaining eggs and then the remaining sauce. Sprinkle on the cheese and bread crumbs. Bake until the top is lightly golden, about 20 minutes. Let rest for 15 minutes before serving.

Serves 6

Green Beans with Tomatoes and Ham

1 lb (500 g) young, tender green beans, trimmed and cut into 2-inch (5-cm) lengths

3 tablespoons olive oil

⅔ cup (2½ oz/75 g) chopped yellow onion

2 cloves garlic, minced

4–5 oz (125–155 g) *presunto (see note)* or prosciutto, chopped

3 cups (18 oz/560 g) peeled, seeded (if desired) and chopped tomatoes *(see glossary, page 107)*

salt and freshly ground pepper

¼ cup (⅓ oz/10 g) chopped fresh flat-leaf (Italian) parsley

In the Mediterranean, green beans are generally cooked until they are quite tender. In this Spanish recipe, they are combined with sautéed onion, garlic and tomatoes and flavored with presunto, the country's famous cured ham. Italian prosciutto can be used in its place.

🌿

*F*ill a saucepan three-fourths full with water, salt it lightly and bring to a boil over high heat. Add the green beans and boil until tender-crisp, about 4 minutes. Drain and immerse in a bowl of cold water to halt the cooking. Drain and set aside.

In a large sauté pan over medium heat, warm the olive oil. Add the onion and sauté, stirring occasionally, until tender, 8–10 minutes. Add the garlic and *presunto* or prosciutto and cook for 1–2 minutes to release their flavors.

Add the drained green beans and tomatoes and bring to a simmer over medium heat. Cover, reduce the heat to low and cook until the tomatoes have thickened and the beans are soft, about 20 minutes. Season to taste with salt and pepper. Transfer to a serving dish and sprinkle with the parsley. Serve hot or at room temperature.

Serves 4–6

Turkish Chicken Pilaf

FOR THE CHICKEN:

1 chicken, 2½–3 lb (1–1.5 kg)

2 carrots, cut into pieces

2 yellow onions, cut into pieces

3 fresh flat-leaf (Italian) parsley sprigs

6 peppercorns

2 cups (14 oz/440 g) long-grain white
  rice, preferably basmati

6 tablespoons (3 oz/90 g) unsalted butter

¼ cup (1 oz/30 g) pine nuts, almonds
  or pistachios

1 cup (4 oz/125 g) chopped yellow onion

¼ teaspoon ground allspice

2 teaspoons salt

freshly ground pepper

¼ cup (1½ oz/45 g) dried currants

pinch of saffron threads, crushed and
  steeped in 2–3 tablespoons water or
  stock (optional)

¼ cup (⅓ oz/10 g) chopped fresh flat-leaf
  (Italian) parsley or dill, plus fresh
  parsley or dill sprigs for garnish

To cook the chicken, place in a stockpot along with the carrots, onions, parsley and peppercorns. Add water to cover and bring to a boil. Using a large spoon, skim off any scum on the surface of the liquid. Reduce the heat to low, cover and simmer until the chicken is tender and the juices run clear when a thigh is pierced at the thickest part with a knife, about 45 minutes.

Transfer the chicken to a plate and let cool. Reserve the stock. Remove the skin and bones and discard. Tear the meat into bite-sized pieces. You should have 1½–2 cups (9–12 oz/280–375 g) meat. Cover and set aside. Strain the stock and set aside 3 cups (24 fl oz/750 ml) for the pilaf. Reserve the remainder for another use.

Place the rice in a fine-mesh sieve and rinse well under cold running water. Transfer to a bowl and add water to cover; let stand for 15 minutes. Drain well.

In a heavy sauté pan over medium heat, melt 3 tablespoons of the butter. Add the nuts and sauté, stirring occasionally, until golden, 4–5 minutes. Transfer the nuts to a plate.

Add the remaining 3 tablespoons butter to the same pan and place over medium heat. Add the onion and sauté until tender, 8–10 minutes. Stir in the allspice, salt and pepper to taste. Add the rice and stir until the grains turn opaque, 3–4 minutes. Stir in the currants, the reserved 3 cups (24 fl oz/750 ml) stock and the saffron, if using. Bring to a boil over medium-high heat. Reduce the heat to low, cover and simmer until nearly all of the liquid is absorbed, 10–15 minutes. Fold in the nuts, reserved chicken, and chopped parsley or dill. Cover tightly, reduce the heat to very low and cook until the liquid is absorbed and the rice is tender, 15–20 minutes longer.

To serve, spoon onto a warmed platter and garnish with parsley or dill sprigs.

Serves 4

Baked Vegetables with Oregano and Dill

1 eggplant (aubergine), about 1 lb (500 g), cut into ½-inch (12-mm) cubes

1½ lb (750 g) zucchini (courgettes), cut into slices ⅓ inch (9 mm) thick

salt

½ cup (4 fl oz/125 ml) olive oil

2 large yellow onions, chopped

5 cloves garlic, minced

6 green (spring) onions, including tender green tops, chopped

3 cups (18 oz/560 g) peeled, seeded and diced tomatoes (see glossary, page 107)

freshly ground pepper

1½ lb (750 g) potatoes, peeled and cut into slices ¼ inch (6 mm) thick

2 green bell peppers (capsicums), seeded, deribbed and diced or sliced

1 tablespoon dried oregano

3 tablespoons chopped fresh dill

¼ cup (⅓ oz/10 g) chopped fresh flat-leaf (Italian) parsley

½ cup (4 fl oz/125 ml) water, or as needed

½ cup (2 oz/60 g) toasted bread crumbs (recipe on page 12)

Easy to prepare, this Greek side dish, called briam, *can be served hot or at room temperature. Some versions include sautéing the eggplant before combining it with other vegetables, but it is an unnecessary step. Other versions leave out the eggplant altogether.*

Sprinkle the eggplant and zucchini with salt and place in a colander. Let stand for 30 minutes to drain off the bitter juices and excess water. Rinse off the salt and dry well with paper towels.

Preheat an oven to 350°F (180°C). Oil a shallow 3-qt (3-l) baking dish with a lid.

In a large sauté pan over medium heat, warm the olive oil. Add the yellow onions and sauté, stirring occasionally, until tender, about 8 minutes. Add the garlic and green onions and sauté, stirring occasionally, for 3 minutes. Add the tomatoes and simmer for 2 minutes to blend the flavors. Season to taste with salt and pepper. Remove from the heat.

Place the eggplant, zucchini, potatoes and bell peppers in a large bowl. Add the contents of the sauté pan and the oregano, dill and parsley. Toss to mix well. Transfer to the prepared baking dish and drizzle evenly with the ½ cup (4 fl oz/125 ml) water. Sprinkle the bread crumbs evenly over the top.

Cover and bake for 30 minutes. Uncover and continue to bake until all the vegetables are tender when pierced with a fork, about 1 hour longer. Check periodically to see if the mixture is drying out, and add water as needed.

Remove from the oven and let cool briefly before serving or serve at room temperature.

Serves 6

Spaghetti alla Puttanesca

6 anchovy fillets

3 tablespoons extra-virgin olive oil

1 tablespoon minced garlic, or to taste

1–2 teaspoons red pepper flakes

2 cups (16 fl oz/500 ml) tomato sauce
(recipe on page 13)

2 tablespoons drained capers, rinsed
and coarsely chopped

¼ cup (⅓ oz/10 g) fresh basil, cut into
thin strips

20 Mediterranean-style black olives,
preferably Gaeta, pitted and quartered
or sliced

salt and freshly ground pepper

1 lb (500 g) dried spaghetti

A specialty of the Campania region, this pasta probably appears on every restaurant menu in Naples. Puttana is Italian slang for "harlot," and this pasta dish is said to be as spicy as a lady of the evening. The Italians do not serve cheese with this dish because of the anchovy, but some people may want grated pecorino on top. If fresh basil is not available, substitute 2 teaspoons dried oregano and add with the red pepper flakes.

In a small food processor, process the anchovy fillets to a purée; you should have about 1 heaping tablespoon. (Alternatively, pound in a mortar with a pestle or crush in a small bowl using a fork.)

In a sauté pan over low heat, warm the olive oil. Add the 1 tablespoon garlic and the anchovy and cook until softened, about 3 minutes. Then add 1 teaspoon of the red pepper flakes. Stir in the tomato sauce and simmer, uncovered, until slightly thickened, about 5 minutes. Add the capers, basil and olives, and simmer until slightly thickened, about 5 minutes longer. Season to taste with salt and pepper and more red pepper flakes, if desired.

Meanwhile, fill a large pot three-fourths full with water, salt it lightly and bring to a boil over high heat. Add the spaghetti, stir well and cook until *al dente* (tender but firm to the bite), about 8 minutes or according to package directions.

If the sauce has finished cooking and has cooled a bit, reheat gently. Drain the pasta and place in a warmed bowl. Add the sauce, toss well and serve at once.

Serves 4–6

Saffron Rice with Seafood

6 cups (48 fl oz/1.5 l) fish stock or half
  water and half bottled clam juice
¼ cup (2 fl oz/60 ml) olive oil
3 cloves garlic, minced
1 yellow onion, minced
salt and freshly ground pepper
1 cup (6 oz/185 g) peeled, seeded and
  diced tomatoes (see glossary, page 107)
  or 3 tablespoons tomato paste
1 teaspoon paprika
¼ teaspoon saffron threads, crushed
  and steeped in 2–3 tablespoons stock
  or water
2 cups (14 oz/440 g) short-grain white
  Spanish rice or Arborio rice
½ lb (250 g) monkfish or other firm
  white fish fillets, cut into 1½-inch
  (4-cm) pieces
½ lb (250 g) shrimp (prawns), peeled
  and deveined (see glossary, page 107)
1½ lb (750 g) mussels, debearded and
  well scrubbed
2 red bell peppers (capsicums), roasted
  and peeled (see glossary, page 104), then
  cut into long strips ¼ inch (6 mm) wide

Called arroz a la marinera, *this seafood version of paella is eaten along the Mediterranean coast of Spain. Some recipes call for adding pieces of cooked chorizo sausage and cooked artichokes or asparagus with the fish.*

🌿

*P*our the stock or water and clam juice into a saucepan and bring to a simmer.

In a large sauté pan (or a paella pan, if you have one) over medium heat, warm the olive oil. Add the garlic, onion and salt and pepper to taste and sauté, stirring, until softened, about 5 minutes. Add the tomatoes or tomato paste, paprika and saffron and its soaking liquid. Cook, stirring, for 3–4 minutes. Add the rice and mix well with the oil. Pour in 5 cups (40 fl oz/1.25 ml) of the hot stock, reduce the heat to low and simmer, uncovered, until the rice is half-cooked, about 10 minutes. Add the remaining 1 cup (8 fl oz/250 ml) stock and the fish pieces, shrimp and mussels (discard any that do not close tightly when touched) and sprinkle with salt. Cook, uncovered, for 10 minutes longer. Taste and adjust the seasonings.

Arrange the mussels (discard any that did not open) and the roasted pepper strips on top of the rice. Cover and leave on the stove top over very low heat for 5–10 minutes to allow all the stock to be fully absorbed. Serve hot.

Serves 4

Linguine with Clams

6 dozen manila clams or 3–4 dozen
   larger hard-shell clams, well scrubbed
1 cup (8 fl oz/250 ml) dry white wine
1 lb (500 g) dried linguine
½ cup (4 fl oz/125 ml) extra-virgin
   olive oil
4 teaspoons finely minced garlic
2 teaspoons dried oregano, optional
pinch of red pepper flakes, optional
2 cups (12 oz/375 g) peeled, seeded and
   diced tomatoes, optional (*see glossary,
   page 107*)
½ cup (¾ oz/20 g) chopped fresh flat-leaf
   (Italian) parsley
freshly ground black pepper
salt
3 tablespoons extra-virgin olive oil or
   3–4 tablespoons unsalted butter,
   optional

When you order pasta with clams—linguine alle vongole—in Italy, the clams are usually tiny and served in the shell. Here, small or large clams can be used and are removed from their shells. For a "red" clam sauce, add the tomatoes; for a "white" clam sauce, leave them out.

Discard any clams with opened or cracked shells. Place the clams in a large, wide saucepan, add the wine, cover and place over high heat. Cook, shaking the pan occasionally, until the clams open, about 5 minutes. Using a slotted spoon, transfer the clams to a colander or bowl; discard any clams that did not open and reserve the cooking liquid. When cool enough to handle, remove the clams from their shells. If they are small, place in a small bowl; if they are large, chop into bite-sized pieces and place in a small bowl. Position a sieve lined with cheesecloth (muslin) over a bowl and pour the reserved liquid through it. Add the liquid to the clams.

Fill a large pot three-fourths full with water, salt it lightly and bring to a boil over high heat. Add the linguine, stir well and cook until *al dente* (tender but firm to the bite), about 8 minutes or according to package directions.

Meanwhile, in a sauté pan over medium-low heat, warm the ½ cup (4 fl oz/125 ml) olive oil. Add the garlic and the oregano and red pepper flakes, if using, and cook to release their fragrance, about 2 minutes. Add the clams and their reserved liquid and the tomatoes, if using. Heat through gently; do not overcook or the clams will toughen. Add the parsley and a generous amount of black pepper. Taste and season with salt, if needed. Swirl in the 3 tablespoons olive oil or 3–4 tablespoons butter, if using.

Drain the pasta and place in a warmed bowl. Add the sauce, toss well and serve at once.

Serves 4–6

Baked Tomatoes with Garlic, Parsley and Bread Crumbs

6 large, ripe but firm tomatoes
salt
6 tablespoons (3 fl oz/90 ml) olive oil
freshly ground pepper
½ cup (2 oz/60 g) fine dried bread crumbs
3 cloves garlic, minced
½ cup (¾ oz/20 g) chopped fresh flat-leaf
   (Italian) parsley

For this Provençal dish, you need ripe, flavorful tomatoes. The key to success is to drain the excess water from the tomato halves so that during baking the tops become crusty and the sides do not split.

❧

Cut the tomatoes in half crosswise. Sprinkle the cut sides with salt and drain, cut sides down, in a colander for about 10 minutes. Dry well with paper towels.

Preheat an oven to 400°F (200°C). Select a baking dish large enough to hold all of the tomato halves in a single layer. Oil the dish lightly.

In a large sauté pan over medium-high heat, warm 2 tablespoons of the olive oil. Add half of the tomato halves, cut sides down, and fry until golden, 3–5 minutes. Transfer to the prepared dish, cut sides up. Repeat with the remaining tomato halves and 2 additional tablespoons olive oil.

Sprinkle the tomatoes with salt and pepper to taste. In a small bowl, stir together the bread crumbs, garlic and a little of the parsley. Spread the mixture on top of the tomatoes, dividing it evenly. Drizzle evenly with the remaining 2 tablespoons oil.

Bake until puffed and juicy, 10–15 minutes. Transfer to a warmed platter or individual plates and sprinkle with the remaining parsley. Serve at once.

Serves 6

Baked Figs with Zabaglione

24 small or 12 large ripe figs
¼ cup (3 oz/90 g) honey
½ cup (4 fl oz/125 ml) fresh orange juice
¼ cup (2 fl oz/60 ml) fresh lemon juice
¼ cup (2 fl oz/60 ml) anisette, optional
4 small bay leaves or fresh lemon balm
  sprigs
3 or 4 thin lemon or orange zest strips

FOR THE ZABAGLIONE:
1 cup (8 fl oz/250 ml) dry Marsala wine
7 egg yolks
½ cup (4 oz/125 g) sugar
grated zest of 1 orange or lemon, optional

6 orange or lemon zest strips, optional

For this recipe, choose either green Adriatic or black Mission figs; they should be ripe and feel heavy in your hand. The zabaglione gives the dish a wonderful Italian accent.

*P*reheat an oven to 350°F (180°C).

Prick the figs in a few places with a fork so they can absorb the cooking juices. Arrange them upright in a baking dish in which they fit snugly. In a small bowl, whisk together the honey and orange and lemon juices and the anisette, if using. Pour over the figs. If necessary, add a little water so that the liquid covers the bottom of the dish by a depth of about ¼ inch (6 mm). Tuck the bay leaves or lemon balm sprigs and 3 or 4 lemon or orange zest strips around the figs.

Cover and bake, basting occasionally with the pan juices, until soft and slightly puffy, 25–35 minutes. Remove from the oven and let cool slightly.

While the figs are cooling, make the zabaglione: In a heatproof bowl, whisk together the Marsala, egg yolks and sugar and the grated orange or lemon zest, if using, until foamy. Set the bowl over, but not touching, gently simmering water. Whisk constantly until very thick, pale and frothy, 10–15 minutes. (If you doubt your stamina, use a handheld electric mixer set on medium speed.)

Place the warm figs on individual plates, dividing evenly. Spoon the cooking juices over them. Top with the warm zabaglione, garnish with zest strips, if desired, and serve at once.

Serves 6

Crème Caramel

FOR THE CARAMEL:
¾ cup (6 oz/185 g) sugar
3 tablespoons water

FOR THE CUSTARD:
3 cups (24 fl oz/750 ml) milk or 1½ cups
   (12 fl oz/375 ml) each milk and light
   cream (single cream)
½ cup (4 oz/125 g) sugar
3 whole eggs, plus 3 egg yolks
1 teaspoon vanilla extract (essence)

*The custard must be made ahead of time and chilled well in order
to unmold it easily. This French classic is comfort food at its best.*

❧

Preheat an oven to 325°F (165°C). Arrange eight 1-cup (8-fl oz/
250-ml) or ten ¾-cup (6-fl oz/180-ml) custard cups in a
baking pan.

   To make the caramel, combine the sugar and water in a small,
heavy saucepan over high heat, stirring to dissolve the sugar.
Bring to a boil and cook without stirring until the sugar turns
a dark golden brown, about 8 minutes. Remove from the heat
and carefully pour into the cups, swirling each cup to coat the
bottom and sides with the caramel. Return to the baking pan.

   To make the custard, mix the milk or milk and cream and
sugar in a saucepan and place over medium heat. Heat, stirring
to dissolve the sugar, until small bubbles appear along the sides
of the pan. Meanwhile, in a bowl, lightly whisk together the
whole eggs and egg yolks until blended. Very gradually add the
hot milk mixture to the eggs, whisking constantly. Whisk in
the vanilla. Transfer the custard to a pitcher and pour into the
caramel-lined cups, dividing it evenly. (If desired, pour through
a fine-mesh sieve to remove any lumps.) Pour very hot water
into the baking pan to reach halfway up the sides of the cups.
Cover the pan with aluminum foil.

   Bake the custards until set and a knife inserted into the center
comes out clean, about 50 minutes. Remove the custards from
the baking pan and place in the refrigerator; chill for at least
3 hours, or cover and chill for up to 2 days.

   To serve, run a knife around the edge of each custard and
turn it out into a small plate or bowl, allowing the caramel in the
bottom of the cup to drizzle over the top of the custard.

Serves 8 or 10

Almond Custard Filo Pastry

1 lb (500 g) almond paste, at room
temperature

½ cup (4 oz/125 g) sugar

8 eggs

2 teaspoons all-purpose (plain) flour

1½ teaspoons baking powder

½ teaspoon ground cinnamon

3 tablespoons brandy

1 tablespoon finely grated orange zest

16 sheets filo dough (about ½ lb/250 g),
thawed in the refrigerator if frozen

½ cup (4 oz/125 g) unsalted butter,
clarified (*see page 8*) and kept warm

FOR THE SYRUP:

2 cups (16 oz/500 g) sugar

1 cup (8 fl oz/250 ml) water

2 tablespoons fresh lemon juice

1 orange zest strip, about 3 inches
(7.5 cm) long and ½ inch (12 mm)
wide

1 cinnamon stick, about 2 inches
(5 cm) long

*P*reheat an oven to 325°F (165°C).

In a bowl, combine the almond paste and sugar. Beat with an
electric mixer set on medium speed until well combined, about
5 minutes. Beat in the eggs one at a time, beating well after each
addition. Add the flour, baking powder, cinnamon, brandy and
orange zest and continue to beat until the mixture is creamy,
about 5 minutes.

Place the filo sheets flat on a work surface. Keep covered with
plastic wrap to prevent them from drying out. Brush the bottom
of an 11-by-16-by-2½-inch (28-by-40-by-6-cm) baking pan
with a little of the warm clarified butter. Lay 1 filo sheet in the
pan and brush lightly with butter. Top the sheet with 7 more
sheets, brushing each with butter. If necessary, cut the sheets
to fit as directed on page 8. Pour in the almond mixture,
spreading it evenly. Layer the remaining 8 filo sheets on top,
again brushing each with butter. Using a sharp knife, score
the top few layers of filo into 16–24 diamonds or squares.
Bake until golden, 45–50 minutes.

Meanwhile, prepare the syrup: In a heavy saucepan over high
heat, combine the sugar, water, lemon juice, orange zest and
cinnamon stick. Bring to a boil, stirring to dissolve the sugar.
Reduce the heat to medium-low and simmer until the syrup is
slightly thickened, 8–10 minutes. Let cool and remove and
discard the orange zest and cinnamon stick.

When done, remove the pastry from the oven. Immediately
pour the cooled syrup evenly over the top. Return to the oven
for 2–3 minutes. Remove and let stand for a few hours before
serving. Using a sharp knife, cut the pastry into pieces along the
scored lines, being careful to cut all the way through to the pan
bottom. Serve at room temperature. Store leftover pastries,
covered, at room temperature for up to 2 days.

Makes 16–24 pieces

Orange Compote with Fragrant Syrup

6 large oranges

1½ cups (12 oz/375 g) sugar

½ cup (4 fl oz/125 ml) water

1 cinnamon stick, about 2 inches (5 cm) long

¼ cup (3 oz/90 g) honey

3 tablespoons orange flower water

3–4 tablespoons slivered blanched almonds or coarsely chopped pistachio nuts, toasted (*see glossary, page 106*), or 3 tablespoons chopped fresh mint leaves (optional)

This dessert would be at home in Turkey, Greece, North Africa and Provence. The orange segments, in a syrup perfumed with orange flower water and cinnamon, should be served well chilled.

❧

Using a vegetable peeler, remove the zest from the oranges. Trim away any bitter white pith from the zest, then cut the zest into very narrow strips. Set aside. Working with 1 orange at a time, cut a thick slice off the top and bottom to remove the pith and membrane and reveal the fruit. Placing the orange upright on a work surface, cut off the peel in thick, wide strips, removing all the white membrane and pith. Cut along both sides of each segment to free it from the membrane, letting the segments drop into a heatproof bowl. Cover and refrigerate.

Bring a small saucepan three-fourths full of water to a boil. Add the zest and boil for 5 minutes. Drain and immerse in cold water to halt the cooking. Drain and set aside.

In a heavy saucepan over high heat, combine the sugar, water, cinnamon stick and honey. Bring to a boil, stirring to dissolve the sugar. Cook briskly until the syrup is quite thick and registers 230°F (110°C) on a candy thermometer, or until it forms 2-inch (5-cm) threads when a tiny bit is dropped into ice water; this should take 10–15 minutes. Remove from the heat and remove and discard the cinnamon stick. Add the reserved orange zest and the orange flower water and pour the syrup over the orange segments. Cover and chill for about 4 hours.

To serve, spoon into individual bowls and garnish with nuts or mint, if desired.

Serves 6

Walnut Cake

FOR THE SYRUP:

¾ cup (6 oz/185 g) sugar

½ cup (6 oz/185 g) honey

1 cup (8 fl oz/250 ml) water

4 whole cloves

1 cinnamon stick, about 2 inches (5 cm) long

1 lemon zest strip, about 2 inches (5 cm) long and ½ inch (12 mm) wide

2 tablespoons fresh lemon juice

FOR THE CAKE:

½ cup (4 oz/125 g) unsalted butter, at room temperature

½ cup (4 oz/125 g) sugar

8 eggs, separated

½ cup (2½ oz/75 g) all-purpose (plain) flour

2 teaspoons baking powder

2 teaspoons ground cinnamon

¼ teaspoon ground cloves

pinch of salt

2½ cups (10 oz/315 g) ground walnuts (see glossary, page 106)

1 tablespoon finely grated orange zest

This light and delicate Greek nut torte is ideal to serve with a fruit dessert such as orange compote with fragrant syrup (recipe on page 96) or baked figs with zabaglione (page 91) or with a little sweetened plain yogurt or whipped cream.

*T*o make the syrup, in a heavy saucepan over medium heat, combine the sugar, honey and water. Bring to a simmer, stirring to dissolve the sugar, then add the cloves, cinnamon stick and lemon zest and juice. Reduce the heat to medium-low and simmer until the syrup is slightly thickened, about 10 minutes. Remove from the heat and set aside to cool.

To make the cake, preheat an oven to 350°F (180°C). Lightly butter a 9-by-12-by-3-inch (23-by-30-by-7.5-cm) cake pan, then dust with flour; tap out the excess.

In a large bowl, using an electric mixer set on high speed, beat together the butter and sugar until light and fluffy, 5–8 minutes. Add the egg yolks one at a time, beating well after each addition. In another bowl, sift together the flour, baking powder, cinnamon, cloves and salt. Gradually fold the flour mixture into the butter mixture, then fold in the nuts and orange zest.

In a large bowl, using clean, dry beaters, beat the egg whites until stiff peaks form. Stir one-third of the whites into the batter, then, using a rubber spatula, fold in the remaining whites just until no white streaks remain. Pour into the prepared pan.

Bake until golden brown and the top springs back when lightly touched, about 45 minutes. Remove from the oven and pour the cooled syrup evenly over the top. Let cool in the pan.

To serve, cut into diamonds or squares.

Makes one 9-by-12-inch (23-by-30-cm) cake; serves 12–16

Poached Pears Stuffed with Cheese and Hazelnuts

juice of 1 lemon

6 ripe but firm Bosc or Winter Nellis pears

zest of 1 lemon

zest of 1 orange

1 cinnamon stick, about 2 inches (5 cm) long

1 cup (8 oz/250 g) sugar

½ cup (4 fl oz/125 ml) water

3 cups (24 fl oz/750 ml) dry white wine

FOR THE FILLING:

¼ lb (125 g) mild Gorgonzola dolcelatte cheese or other mild and crumbly blue-veined cheese such as Cambozola

1 cup (8 oz/250 g) mascarpone cheese

¼ cup (1½ oz/45 g) hazelnuts (filberts), toasted and peeled (see glossary, page 106), then chopped

The most popular dessert in the Mediterranean is a selection of ripe fruits paired with an assortment of local cheeses. This dish combines the two by stuffing a cheese-and-nut mixture into poached pears. Dry red wine can be used in place of the white wine.

Have ready a large bowl three-fourths full of water to which you have added the lemon juice. Peel the pears. Cut in half lengthwise and cut out the cores. As the pears are cored, slip them into the bowl of lemon water to prevent darkening.

In a wide, deep saucepan over high heat, combine the lemon and orange zests, cinnamon stick, sugar, water and wine. Bring to a boil, stirring to dissolve the sugar. Drain the pears and add to the saucepan. Reduce the heat to low and cook gently, uncovered, until a skewer or the tip of a knife penetrates the pears easily, about 30 minutes. Using a slotted spoon, transfer to a bowl. Raise the heat to high and cook the liquid until reduced to a medium-thick syrup, 8–10 minutes. Remove from the heat and pour through a fine-mesh sieve into a heatproof bowl; discard the zest strips and cinnamon stick. Let the pears and syrup cool. Cover and refrigerate the pears and the syrup separately until well chilled, about 3 hours.

To make the filling, crumble the Gorgonzola or other cheese into a bowl and mash well with a fork. Add the mascarpone and nuts and mix well. Cover and chill along with the pears and syrup.

To serve, stuff the pear halves with the cheese filling, dividing it evenly. Place on individual plates. Spoon the chilled syrup around the pears and serve at once.

Serves 6

Cherry Clafouti

1½ lb (750 g) Bing cherries, pitted
1½ cups (12 fl oz/375 ml) milk
4 eggs
½ cup (2½ oz/75 g) all-purpose (plain)
  flour
⅓ cup (3 oz/90 g) granulated sugar
2 teaspoons vanilla extract (essence)
2 tablespoons kirsch or amaretto
confectioners' (icing) sugar

Tiny, dark, sweet cherries are a specialty of the Limousin region of France, where this dessert originates. A few tablespoons of chopped candied ginger can be added with the cherries. For ease of entertaining, arrange the fruit in the baking dish ahead of time and have the batter ingredients ready. Then you need only to blend, pour and bake.

Preheat an oven to 350°F (180°C). Butter a shallow 1½-qt (1.5-l) baking dish or wide gratin dish or a 10-inch (25-cm) pie pan. It must be deep enough for the batter almost to cover the cherries.

Spread the cherries on the bottom of the prepared dish or pan. Just before you are ready to bake the clafouti, combine the milk, eggs, flour, granulated sugar, vanilla and kirsch or amaretto in a blender or in a food processor fitted with the metal blade. Process for 1 minute. Stop the machine and scrape down the sides of the container, then process again until no lumps remain. Pour the batter over the cherries.

Bake until the top is golden brown and a knife inserted into the center comes out clean, 45–60 minutes. Remove from the oven and, using a fine-mesh sieve or a sifter, dust the top with confectioners' sugar. Serve very warm.

Serves 6

Glossary

The following glossary defines terms both generally and as they relate specifically to Mediterranean cooking, including major and unusual ingredients and basic techniques.

ANCHOVIES
Tiny saltwater fish, related to sardines. Imported anchovy fillets packed in olive oil are the most commonly available. Whole anchovies packed in salt, available canned in some Italian delicatessens, are considered the finest.

BELL PEPPERS
Sweet-fleshed, bell-shaped members of the pepper family, also known as capsicums. Most commonly sold in the unripe green form, although ripened red or yellow varieties are also available.

To prepare a raw bell pepper, cut it in half lengthwise with a sharp knife. Pull out the stem section from each half, along with the cluster of seeds attached to it. Remove any remaining seeds, along with any thin white membranes, or ribs, to which they are attached. Cut the pepper halves as directed in specific recipes.

To roast bell peppers, preheat a broiler (griller). Cut the bell peppers lengthwise into quarters, then remove the stems, seeds and ribs as directed above. Place the pepper quarters, cut side down, on a broiler pan and broil until the skins blister and blacken. Remove from the broiler, cover with aluminum foil and let stand until the peppers soften and are cool enough to handle, about 10 minutes. Using your fingertips or a small knife, peel off the blackened skins. Then tear or cut the peppers as directed in the recipe.

BEANS AND LENTILS
Dried beans and lentils, whether cooked at home from scratch or precooked and canned, are a staple of Mediterranean kitchens. Those used in this book are among the most common varieties.
Cannellini Italian variety of small to medium, white, thin-skinned oval beans. Great Northern or white kidney beans may be substituted.
Chick-peas Round, tan member of the pea family, with a slightly crunchy texture and nutlike flavor. Also known as garbanzo beans or ceci beans.
Lentils Small, disk-shaped dried legumes, prized for their rich, earthy flavor when cooked. The most commonly sold types are brown lentils, which have brownish green skins, and red lentils, a variety from which the skins have been removed, revealing a pale orange flesh.
White Beans Thin-skinned oval beans ranging from small white (navy) and *Cannellini* beans to larger Great Northern and white kidney beans.

BREAD, COARSE COUNTRY
For serving with authentic Mediterranean dishes and for making toasts and bread crumbs, choose a good-quality, rustic loaf made from unbleached wheat flour, with a firm, coarse-textured crumb. Sold in bakeries and well-stocked food stores, such loaves may be referred to by any of several terms, including "country style," "rustic" or "peasant."

BREAD CRUMBS, DRIED
Dried bread crumbs have many uses: they add body to stuffings, form a coating for fried foods and create a crunchy golden topping on baked dishes.

To make crumbs, choose a good-quality **coarse country bread.** Cut away the crusts and crumble the bread by hand or in a blender or a food processor fitted with the metal blade. Spread the crumbs on a baking sheet, place in an oven set at its lowest temperature and dry slowly, about 1 hour. Store in a covered container at room temperature. Dried bread crumbs, usually fine textured, are also sold prepackaged in food stores.

CAPERS
Small, pickled buds of a bush common to the Mediterranean, used whole or chopped as a savory flavoring or garnish.

CHEESES
Whether featured in a recipe or used as a garnish or seasoning, cheese appears frequently in Mediterranean cuisine. Cheeses used in this book include:

Feta White, salty, sharp-tasting cheese made from sheep's or goat's milk, with a crumbly, somewhat creamy consistency.
Gorgonzola Dolcelatte Literally "sweet milk Gorgonzola," this is a mild, creamy variety of the familiar Italian blue-veined cheese.
Mascarpone A thick Italian cream cheese, similar to French crème fraîche and usually sold in tubs. Look for mascarpone in the cheese case of an Italian delicatessen or a specialty-food shop.
Mozzarella Rindless white, mild-tasting Italian cheese traditionally made from water buffalo's milk and, in Italy and in Italian delicatessens, often sold fresh, immersed in water. Commercially produced and packaged cow's milk mozzarella has a lower moisture content, which gives it better melting properties for cooked dishes.
Parmesan Hard, thick-crusted Italian cow's milk cheese with a sharp, salty, full flavor resulting from at least two years of aging. The finest Italian variety is designated Parmigiano-Reggiano®. Buy in block form, to grate fresh as needed.
Pecorino Italian sheep's milk cheese, sold either fresh or aged. Two of its most popular aged forms are pecorino romano and pecorino sardo; the latter is tangier than the former.
Ricotta Light, bland Italian cheese made from twice-cooked milk—traditionally sheep's milk, although cow's milk ricotta is now far more common. Produced from the whey left over from making other cheeses, typically mozzarella and provolone. Freshly made ricotta, available in Italian delicatessens, is particularly prized for its rich flavor and fluffy, creamy texture.

CINNAMON
The aromatic bark of a type of evergreen tree, this sweet spice is sold as whole dried strips—cinnamon sticks—or ground.

CLAM JUICE
The strained liquid of shucked clams, sold in small bottles in the fresh or canned seafood departments of food stores. Because of its refreshing briny flavor, the juice is often used as a cooking liquid for seafood dishes.

COUSCOUS
Sometimes mistakenly thought to be a type of grain, couscous is in fact a tiny pasta made from semolina wheat. Originating in North Africa, it is now popular in northern Mediterranean countries as well. Steamed and served as a base for stews or braises, it is enjoyed for its light, fluffy consistency and mild, nutlike flavor. Authentic couscous can take close to an hour to cook, but many food stores sell an acceptable quick-cooking variety that has been precooked and then redried.

CUMIN
Middle Eastern spice with a strong, dusky, aromatic flavor. Sold ground or as whole, small, crescent-shaped seeds.

EGGPLANTS
Vegetable-fruits, also known as aubergines, with tender, mildly earthy, sweet flesh. The shiny skins of eggplants vary in color from purple to red and from yellow to white, and their shapes range from small and oval to long and slender to large and pear

shaped. The most common variety is the large, purple globe eggplant (below). Slender, purple Asian eggplants, more tender and with fewer, smaller seeds, are available with increasing frequency in food stores and vegetable markets.

FENNEL
Crisp, refreshing, mildly anise-flavored bulb vegetable. Its fine, feathery leaves are used as a fresh or dried herb, and its small, crescent-shaped seeds are dried and used as a spice. Sometimes called by its Italian name, *finocchio*.

FIGS
Late summer and early autumn fruits characterized by their many tiny edible seeds, sweet, slightly astringent flavor and soft, succulent texture—qualities that become intensified when the figs are dried. Among the commonly available varieties are purple-black Missions with soft skins and intensely flavored pink flesh; Calimyrnas, a large California hybrid of the Mediterranean Smyrna fig, with green skin,

white to pale pink flesh and a sweet, nutty flavor; and small, yellowish green Kadotas with sweet purple-pink flesh. Either of the latter two types may be used in recipes calling for the less common Adriatic figs, which have green skin and reddish flesh. It is best to buy fresh figs when fully ripe and to use them immediately.

HERBS
All manner of fresh and dried herbs are added to dishes in Mediterranean kitchens. Among the most common types, used in this book, are:
Basil Sweet, spicy herb popular in Italian and French cooking.
Bay Leaves Pungent, spicy, dried whole leaves of the bay laurel tree. The French variety, sometimes available in specialty-food shops, has a milder, sweeter flavor than California bay leaves. Remove and discard the leaves from a dish before serving it.

Cilantro Green, leafy herb resembling flat-leaf (Italian) **parsley,** with a sharp, aromatic, somewhat astringent flavor. Also called fresh

coriander and referred to as Chinese parsley.
Dill Fine, feathery leaves with a sweet, aromatic flavor. Sold fresh or dried, and used in savory pastries and baked vegetables.

Lemon Balm Sweet, lemon-scented herb, used fresh with fruit and in egg dishes, soups, salads and other sweet and savory dishes.
Mint Refreshing herb available in many varieties, with spearmint the most common. Used fresh to flavor a broad range of savory and sweet preparations.
Oregano Aromatic, pungent and spicy herb—also known as wild marjoram—used fresh or dried as a seasoning for all kinds of savory

dishes. Especially popular with tomatoes and other vegetables.

Parsley This popular fresh herb is available in two varieties, the common curly-leaf type and a flat-leaf type. The latter, also known as Italian parsley (below), has a more pronounced flavor and is preferred, especially in Mediterranean dishes.

Crushing Dried Herbs If using dried herbs, it is best to crush them first in the palm of the hand to release their flavor. Or warm them in a frying pan and crush using a mortar and pestle.

FILO

Tissue-thin sheets of flour-and-water pastry used throughout the Middle East as crisp wrappers for savory or sweet fillings. The name derives from the Greek word for "leaf." Usually found in the frozen-food section of well-stocked food stores or purchased fresh in Middle Eastern delicatessens. Defrost frozen filo thoroughly in the refrigerator before use.

GRAPE LEAVES

In Greek and other Middle Eastern cuisines, grapevine leaves are commonly used as edible wrappers. They are sold bottled in brine in ethnic delicatessens and the specialty-food sections of well-stocked food stores. Rinse gently and remove tough stems before use. If fresh leaves are available, briefly blanch or steam to soften before use.

LEEKS

Long and cylindrical, moderately flavored member of the onion family, with a pale white root end and dark green leaves. Select firm, unblemished leeks, small to medium in size. Grown in sandy soil, the multilayered vegetables require thorough cleaning.

To clean leeks, trim off the roots. Trim off the dark green leaves where they meet the pale green part of the stem. Starting about 1 inch (2.5 cm) from the root end, slit each leek length-wise. Vigorously swish the leek in a basin or sink filled with cold water. Drain and rinse again;

check to make sure that no dirt remains between the tightly packed pale portion of the leaves.

NUTMEG

Popular baking spice that is the hard pit of the fruit of the nutmeg tree. May be bought already ground or, for fresher flavor, whole. Whole nutmegs may be kept inside special nutmeg graters, which include hinged flaps that conceal a storage compartment.

OILS

Not only do oils provide a medium in which foods may be browned without sticking, but they can also subtly enhance the flavor of many dishes. Store all oils in airtight containers away from heat and light. Extra-virgin olive oil, extracted from olives on the first pressing without use of heat or chemicals, is prized for its pure, fruity taste and golden to pale green hue. The higher-priced extra-virgin olive oils are usually of better quality. Products labeled "pure olive oil," less aromatic and flavorful, may be used for all-purpose cooking. For recipes in this book that call for "olive oil," use your choice of extra-virgin or pure. Walnut oil, used in salad dressings and as a seasoning, conveys the rich taste of the nuts from which it is pressed; seek out oil made from lightly toasted nuts, which has a full, though not overpowering flavor.

OLIVES

Good-quality cured black olives are sold in well-stocked food stores and delicatessens. For Mediterranean-style dishes, choose from such varieties as Greek Kalamata (below), which

NUTS

Rich and mellow in flavor, crisp and crunchy in texture, a wide variety of nuts complements Mediterranean recipes. Some of the most popular options include:

Almonds Mellow, sweet-flavored nuts that are an important crop in California and are popular throughout the world. Blanched almonds are those sold with their brown skins removed, leaving just the pale ivory meats. Plain or sweetened almond paste, made by grinding the nuts without or with sugar, is sometimes called for in Mediterranean desserts.

Hazelnuts Spherical nuts with a slightly sweet flavor. Grown in Italy, Spain and the United States. Also known as filberts.

Pine Nuts Small, ivory seeds from the cones of a species of pine tree, with a rich, slightly resinous flavor. Also known by the Italian *pinoli* and, in the American Southwest, by the Spanish *piñones*.

Pistachios Slightly sweet, full-flavored nuts with distinctively green, crunchy meat. Native to Asia Minor, they are grown primarily in the Middle East and California.

Walnuts Rich, crisp-textured nuts with distinctively crinkled surfaces. English walnuts, the most familiar variety, are grown worldwide, although the largest crops are in California.

Toasting Nuts
Preheat an oven to 325°F (165°C). Spread the nuts in a single layer on a baking sheet and toast until fragrant and just beginning to change color, 5–10 minutes. Let cool to room temperature. Toasting loosens the skins of nuts such as hazelnuts and walnuts. Wrap the still-warm nuts in a cotton towel and rub against them with the palms of your hands to remove the skins.

Grinding Nuts
A countertop nut mill is the best tool for grinding nuts evenly, especially to achieve the proper texture for use as a flour. Place the shelled nuts in the top compartment, called a hopper, and turn the hand crank. Alternatively, use a food processor; do not over-process or the nuts will turn into a paste.

are brine cured and packed in vinegar; French Niçoise, small, black, salt-cured olives; Italian Gaeta, small, salt-cured olives; or sun-dried, oil-cured Moroccan olives.

PASTA
Italy's native pasta finds favor throughout Mediterranean kitchens. The following common dried pasta shapes are used in this book:

Linguine "Small tongues." Long, narrow, flat strands.

Macaroni Small to medium, short, curved tubes.

Penne "Quills." Tubes with angled ends, available smooth and ridged.

Rigatoni Moderately sized ridged tubes.

Shells Called *conchiglie* (conch shells) in Italian. Available in various sizes.

Spaghetti Classic long rods.

RICE
Among the many different types of rice grown, milled and cooked around the world, the most popular varieties used in Mediterranean kitchens are:

Arborio Popular Italian variety with short, round grains high in starch, which creates a creamy, saucelike consistency during cooking. Available in Italian delicatessens and well-stocked food stores.

Basmati Long-grain white variety, principally from India, which cooks to form fluffy individual kernels prized for their highly aromatic character.

Short-Grain White Spanish Variety imported from Spain, with short, plump grains resembling Arborio and yielding similarly starchy, chewy results. Particularly suitable for paella.

SHRIMP
Raw shrimp (prawns) are generally sold with the heads already removed but the shells still intact. Before cooking, they are usually peeled and their veinlike intestinal tracts removed. After deveining, large shrimp are frequently butterflied to help them cook more evenly.

To peel and devein shrimp, using your thumbs, split open the shrimp's thin shell along

the concave side, between its two rows of legs. Peel away the shell, taking care to leave the last segment with tail fin intact and attached to the meat if specified in the recipe.

Using a small, sharp knife, carefully make a shallow slit along the peeled shrimp's back, just deep enough to expose the long, thin, usually dark intestinal tract. With the tip of the knife or your fingers, lift up and pull out the vein, discarding it.

SAFFRON
Intensely aromatic, golden orange spice made from the dried stigmas of a species of crocus; used to perfume and color many classic Mediterranean and East Indian dishes. Sold either as threads—the dried stigmas—or in powdered form. Look for products labeled "pure saffron."

SHERRY
Fortified, cask-aged Spanish wine, ranging from dry to sweet, enjoyed as an aperitif and used as a flavoring in both savory dishes and desserts. The driest of sherries are generally known by the designation "fino." Amontillado sherries are noted for their somewhat higher alcohol content and nutlike bouquet. Stronger still are the full-bodied, deep-colored oloroso sherries.

TOMATOES
During summer, when tomatoes are in season, use the best red or yellow sun-ripened tomatoes you can find. At other times of year, plum tomatoes, sometimes called Roma or egg tomatoes, are likely to have the best flavor and texture; for cooking, canned whole, diced, chopped or puréed plum tomatoes are also good.

To peel fresh tomatoes, bring a saucepan of water to a boil. Using a small, sharp knife, cut out the core from the stem end of the tomato. Then cut a shallow X in the skin at the tomato's base. Submerge for about 20 seconds in the boiling water, then remove and cool in a bowl of cold water.

Starting at the X, peel the skin from the tomato, using your fingertips and, if necessary, the knife blade.

Cut the tomato in half and turn each half cut-side down. Cut as directed in individual recipes.

To seed a tomato, cut it in half crosswise. Squeeze gently to force out the seed sacs.

VINEGARS
Literally "sour wine," vinegar results when certain strains of yeast cause wine—or some other alcoholic liquid such as apple cider or Japanese rice wine—to ferment for a second time, turning it acidic. The best-quality wine vinegars begin with good-quality wine. Red wine vinegar, like the wine from which it is made, has a more robust flavor than vinegar produced from white wine. Balsamic vinegar, a specialty of Modena, Italy, is a vinegar made from reduced grape juice and aged for many years.

ZEST
Thin, brightly colored, outermost layer of a citrus fruit's peel, containing most of its aromatic essential oils—a lively source of flavor. It may be removed with a simple tool known as a zester, drawn across the fruit's skin to remove the zest in thin strips; with a fine handheld grater; or in wide strips with a vegetable peeler or a paring knife held almost parallel to the fruit's skin.

Index

ACKNOWLEDGMENTS

The publishers would like to thank the following people for their generous
assistance and support in producing this book: Lorraine and Jud Puckett, Patty
Draper, Patty Hill, Ken DellaPenta, Tina Schmitz, and the buyers and store
managers for Pottery Barn and Williams-Sonoma stores.

The following kindly lent props for the photography:
Biordi Art Imports, Candelier, Sue Fisher King,
Chuck Williams, Williams-Sonoma and Pottery Barn.